The Usborne
Big Book of
Fantasy Quests

Andy Dixon

Illustrated by
Simone Boni & Nick Harris

Edited by
Felicity Brooks

Cover and additional design by Stephanie Jones

Additional editing by Claire Masset

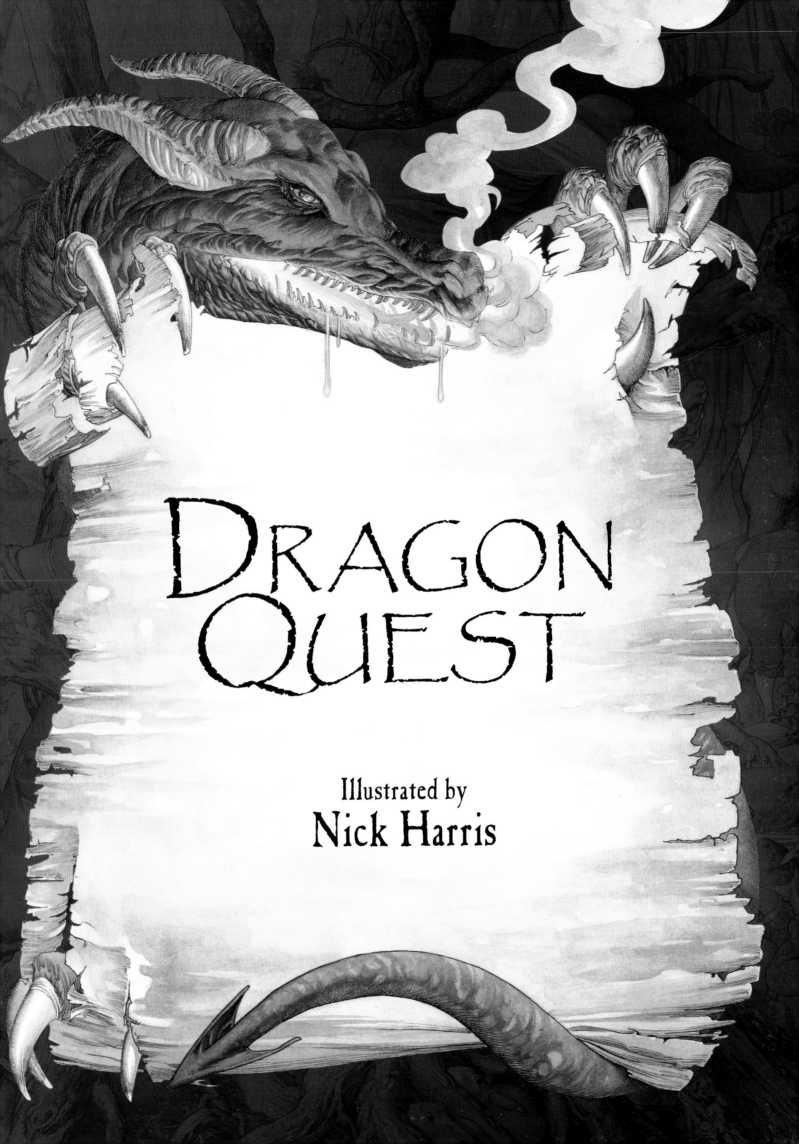

DRAGON QUEST

Illustrated by
Nick Harris

SHORTSVILLE NEEDS
YOU!

Citizens of Shortsville,

Once we were a happy, hairy people who had few problems and led easy lives. We joked and laughed. Our days were filled with joy. Then came the terrible day when a spell was cast over our village, an evil spell that made all our hair disappear! And we all know who was responsible for this callous crime. It was that spiteful, bald creature, Winston, the Wig-wearing Wizard. The time has come to put an end to his reign of terror. We must find and destroy the Well of Spells which is the source of his magic power. The journey will be long and dangerous and the well is guarded by a fearsome, fire-breathing dragon. So, citizens of Shortsville, I am looking for:

VOLUNTEERS TO GO ON THE DRAGON QUEST

If you think you are brave enough to face these challenges, then enter the Shortsville competitions and earn yourself a place on the quest.

Bag P. Dribbet

Mayor of Shortsville

Important information for all questers

Thank you for volunteering to go on the Dragon Quest, and welcome to the Land of Grandos. These are some things you need to know before you set off.

Your present location

You are in Shortsville, a village of little people in the Land of Grandos. The village is in the grip of a powerful spell cast by an evil wizard.

Your enemy

Your enemy is Winston, the Wig-wearing Wizard. He is a jealous and spiteful bald wizard who has recently cast a spell which made all of the villagers' hair fall out.

Your mission

The purpose of the quest is to find and destroy the Well of Spells which gives Winston all his magic power. The spell will be lifted as soon as the well is destroyed.

The Well of Spells

No one in Shortsville knows exactly where the Well of Spells is, but it is known to be guarded by a huge, fearsome dragon.

Your fellow questers

The three winners of the Shortsville competitions will go with you on the Dragon Quest. These competitions have been organized by Bag P. Dribbet, the Mayor of Shortsville. They are starting soon.

Time limit

Winter is approaching. The villagers need their hair to keep warm. Your mission must be accomplished as quickly as possible.

Your route

Your exact route is unknown, but you will set out from Shortsville and visit many other places in Grandos. The map below shows the whole of Grandos. Please study it carefully.

Octopus Ocean

Cadaver Castle

Sailor's Rest

Stinky Swamp

Trog Tower

Wingtip Rock

Misery Wood

Burning Rocks

Woodsman's Island

Shortsville

THE LAND OF
GRANDOS

N

E

S

Old Mine

YOU ARE HERE

Temple
of Fear

Tail End

Doomstones

The parchments

The quest will be difficult and dangerous, so you will need courage, cunning and the eyes of an eagle if you are to survive. In every place you visit you will see a piece of parchment similar to the one below. It contains vital information to get you safely through to the next stage of the quest.

Octopus Ocean

SAMPLE

You've escaped from the ship into Octopus Ocean, where strange sea creatures lurk in every cavern and under every stone. Walking along the seabed is much too dangerous and slow, so you must find a faster and safer way to travel.

Someone has been here before you and left behind a small submarine. If you could make it work, it would be faster than walking, but the propeller is missing. Find the propeller and escape from the sea creatures.

Somewhere in the distance are 3 pipes which are sewer outlets from Cadaver Castle. Only one is safe to enter. The others are in use. Can you find some clues to show you which is the safe outlet?

Octopus Ocean has some of the largest and most valuable pearls in the world. Find 8 pearls. They may be useful later.

Most of the sea creatures are poisonous or too dangerous to catch. The crabs are safe to eat but they may give you a nasty nip. Find 6.

This tells you where you are.

These maps will help to remind you where each place is in Grandos. They come from an ancient book that belongs to the wise old man of Shortsville.

When it is time, read these pieces of information carefully. They contain some very important clues.

The pictures show people or things you have to find or avoid in each place you visit. Some will be very hard to spot, because you can only see a small part of them.

Some pictures show things you will need later in the quest or ways of getting to the next place.

At the bottom of the parchment are pictures of food or drink to look for. You can find something to eat in each place you visit.

The red keys

Hidden in each of the first nine places you visit is one red key. You will need all nine later to help you defeat Winston, so don't forget to look for them.

The squares

At the bottom of each page are some more pictures in squares. The numbers tell you how many of that thing you can spot in the main scene. Finding these things will sharpen your skills and help you survive the quest.

11 seahorses

19 clownfish

The Shortsville competitions are about to begin. Turn the page to find out who will be going with you on the DRAGON QUEST...

Shortsville

The villagers of Shortsville are competing to find three people to go on the Dragon Quest. The judges are looking for people who are wise, brave and strong. The winners will go with you on your journey. Can you find them in the crowd?

Sprag wears glasses and a white shirt. He has a blue hat with spikes on it.

Dig always smiles. He wears a tiny red hat, a striped sweater and a shirt with a big white collar.

Pug wears an orange hat and a pink dress with yellow flowers. She hates ice cream.

To find your way, you'll need the book of maps. The wise old man of Shortsville is carrying it under his left arm. Can you find it?

There are all kinds of hidden dangers in Grandos, so you will need some weapons to protect yourselves. Can you find 4 swords, 2 axes and 2 shields?

You can't fight dragons on an empty stomach. You will need to take some food and drink. Find 7 bottles of yab's milk, 9 big bug burgers, and 9 tasty tarts.

10 snails

7 ice cream cones

9 buckets

22 judges

3 yabs

6 puppets

5 boxing gloves

Misery Wood

Your first stop is Misery Wood, a dark and dangerous place. There are six doors that lead out of the wood, but only one leads to safety. The other five will take you to Trog Tower from which there is no escape. Choose carefully or all is lost, and do not trust the rabbits.

The Trogs live in Trog Tower. They catch rabbits to put in their supper pot, but they prefer dwarves and humans. The Trogs are cowards. They always attack from behind, but if you shout "BOO!" at them, they'll run away. Find all 12 or they'll have you for supper.

The rabbits are mean and miserable creatures. They don't have any friends because they always tell lies. They know which door leads to safety, but when you ask them, they point the wrong way. Can you find all 34 rabbits and the safe door?

There is plenty of food in the woods, if you know what to look for. Find 9 apples, 10 wild mushrooms and fill your bottle from the stream.

9 birds

7 worms

5 moles

7 clubs 7 squirrels 16 flowers 5 owls 8 butterflies

Woodsman's Hut

You've escaped from Misery Wood and found your way to the woodsman's hut. The woodsman is very forgetful and his hut is so untidy that he can never find anything. Some weeks ago he lost something very important – the key to the clock that controls time.

This magical clock controls time in the woodsman's hut. When it stops, time stands still. To restore time, you must first find the clock and then the key to wind it.

☩ Key

Your next stop will be the Stinky Swamp. Many nasty creatures skulk in its murky depths. You need to find a boat and 2 oars to travel through the swamp.

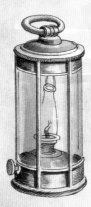

Night is falling fast. The swamp is the darkest place in Grandos. To light your way, you need to find a lantern and 7 candles.

There isn't much food here, but you are welcome to take 7 pieces of cheese. It's so smelly that even the mice won't touch it.

9 socks   9 ducks   6 hammers

6 saws   6 matchboxes   15 mice   6 pencils   7 paintbrushes

Stinky Swamp

Now you're in the middle of the swamp and the Frogmen are attacking your boat! You can't fight them off, so you need to distract them. Pug sees a huge model fly that has crashed in the water. If you can make it work, the Frogmen's frogs will chase it, as flies are the food they like best.

There are some parts missing from the engine in the fly's head. Find 3 batteries and 2 spark plugs to make it work.

The boat is filling up with water! Sprag pulled out the plug and threw it over the side by mistake. Can you find the plug before the boat sinks?

The frogmen keep their gold in the swamp. If you find 12 gold coins, you can hire a ship and its crew to take you to Cadaver Castle, the Wizard's home.

The only nice things in the Stinky Swamp are the purple cherries. Some grow as big as basketballs. There are 8 cherries to find.

6 tadpoles

8 herons

8 otters

9 grubs 9 piranhas 5 skulls 9 snakes 10 terrapins

13

Sailor's Rest

You've arrived at the Sailor's Rest Tavern. It is packed with pirates and other nasty people, all busy drinking, shouting and fighting. Somewhere in the crowd are the captain and crew of *The Serpent*, a pirate ship. If you can find them, they will take you to the Wizard's castle for twelve gold coins.

Captain Mullet wears a large blue pirate hat and an eyepatch. He has a hook on his right arm.

The crew of *The Serpent* all wear the secret anchor and serpent symbol. There are 7 crew members to find somewhere in the room.

Some of the ship's equipment has been stolen and hidden in the tavern. Before the ship can sail, you must find the wheel, the compass and the telescope.

No pirate ship worth its salt will leave port without a pirate flag. Can you spot the flag?

There isn't much that's safe to eat or drink here, except 8 parakeet pies and 8 bottles of berry juice. Can you find them?

10 eyepatches

10 parrots

8 hooks

5 wooden legs | 6 watches | 9 cutlasses | 5 treasure maps | 23 playing cards

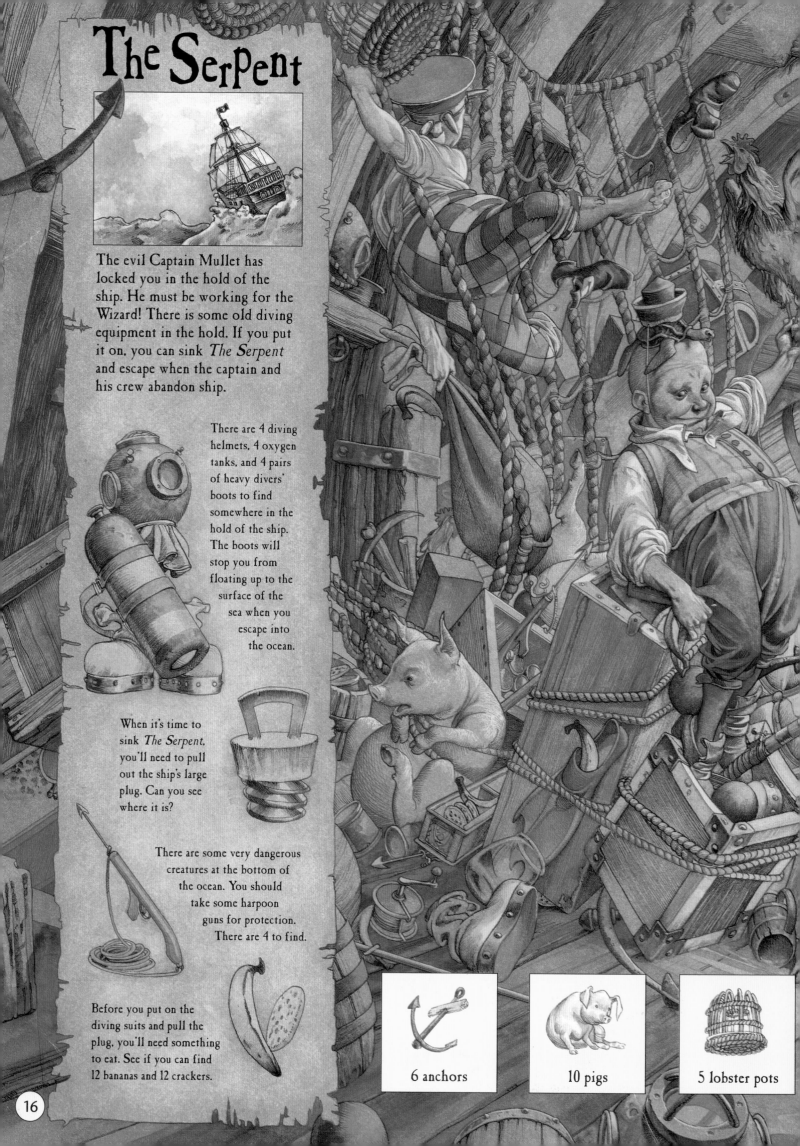

The Serpent

The evil Captain Mullet has locked you in the hold of the ship. He must be working for the Wizard! There is some old diving equipment in the hold. If you put it on, you can sink *The Serpent* and escape when the captain and his crew abandon ship.

There are 4 diving helmets, 4 oxygen tanks, and 4 pairs of heavy divers' boots to find somewhere in the hold of the ship. The boots will stop you from floating up to the surface of the sea when you escape into the ocean.

When it's time to sink *The Serpent*, you'll need to pull out the ship's large plug. Can you see where it is?

There are some very dangerous creatures at the bottom of the ocean. You should take some harpoon guns for protection. There are 4 to find.

Before you put on the diving suits and pull the plug, you'll need something to eat. See if you can find 12 bananas and 12 crackers.

6 anchors

10 pigs

5 lobster pots

10 cannon balls

11 chickens

7 fishing reels

7 barrels

Octopus Ocean

You've escaped from the ship into Octopus Ocean, where strange sea creatures lurk in every cavern and under every stone. Walking along the seabed is much too dangerous and slow, so you must find a faster and safer way to travel.

Someone has been here before you and left a small submarine behind. If you could make it work, it would be faster than walking, but the propeller is missing. Find the propeller and escape from the sea creatures.

Somewhere in the distance are 3 pipes which are sewer outlets from Cadaver Castle. Only one is safe to enter. The others are in use. Can you find some clues to show you which is the safe outlet?

Octopus Ocean has some of the largest and most valuable pearls in the world. Find 8 pearls. They may be useful later.

Most of the sea creatures are poisonous or too dangerous to catch. The crabs are safe to eat, but they may give you a nasty nip. Find 6.

8 octopuses

19 clownfish

6 eels

12 sea urchins

8 sharks

11 seahorses

10 starfish

5 giant clams

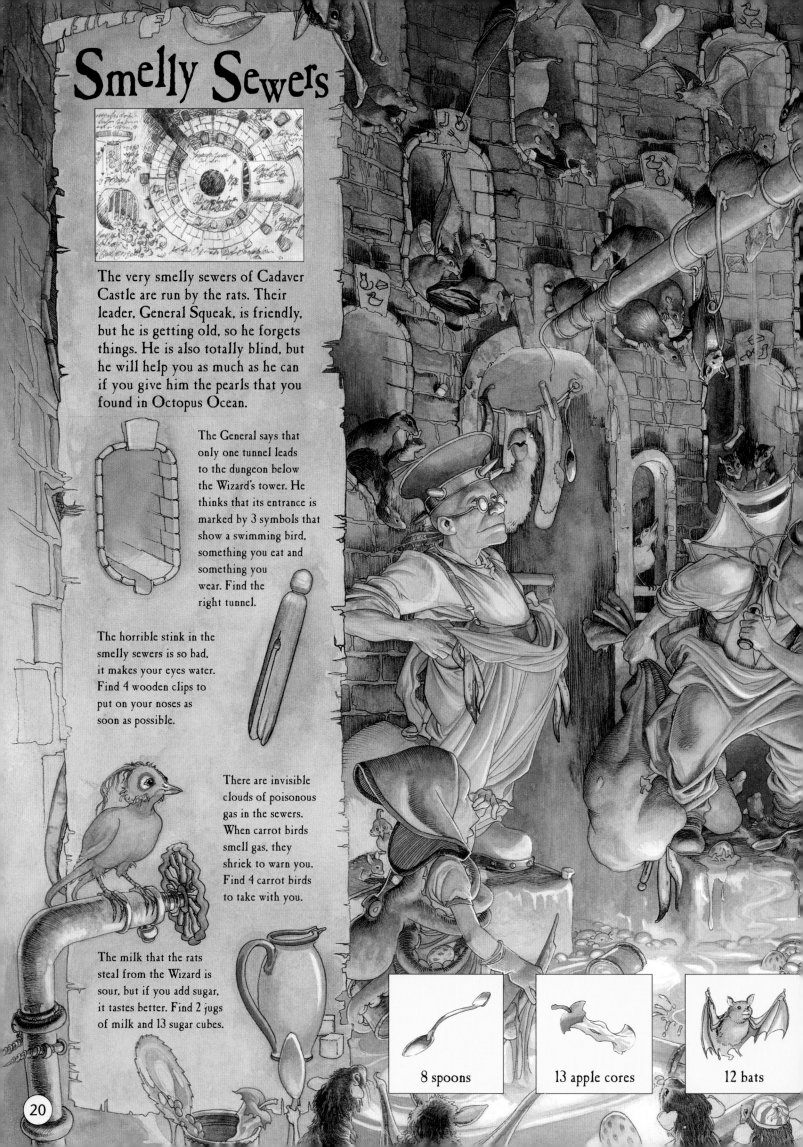

Smelly Sewers

The very smelly sewers of Cadaver Castle are run by the rats. Their leader, General Squeak, is friendly, but he is getting old, so he forgets things. He is also totally blind, but he will help you as much as he can if you give him the pearls that you found in Octopus Ocean.

The General says that only one tunnel leads to the dungeon below the Wizard's tower. He thinks that its entrance is marked by 3 symbols that show a swimming bird, something you eat and something you wear. Find the right tunnel.

The horrible stink in the smelly sewers is so bad, it makes your eyes water. Find 4 wooden clips to put on your noses as soon as possible.

There are invisible clouds of poisonous gas in the sewers. When carrot birds smell gas, they shriek to warn you. Find 4 carrot birds to take with you.

The milk that the rats steal from the Wizard is sour, but if you add sugar, it tastes better. Find 2 jugs of milk and 13 sugar cubes.

8 spoons

13 apple cores

12 bats

11 bones

15 teabags

15 rotten eggs

11 tin cans

19 banana skins

Giant's Kitchen

You've escaped from the smelly sewers into a kitchen, where a giant grabs hold of Pug. He says that he and his wife are exhausted. They've been slaving away all day for the Wizard, who has been ringing for food from his tower. Now they are too tired to make their own supper, but the giant is hungry. He won't let go of Pug unless you make him a hot meal.

The giant wants a mushroom omelette. All the ingredients are somewhere in the kitchen. Find some butter, a bottle of yab's milk, 6 eggs and 9 mushrooms.

The next place you visit will be the Spellroom in the tower. The Wizard has many large and nasty cats. Take some cans of cat food and a can opener to keep them happy. There are 8 cans to find.

There won't be any omelette left for you, but if you are quick you can fry some bacon and tomatoes. There are 7 tomatoes and 7 slices of bacon to find.

To get into the Spellroom without being noticed, you can use the "dumb waiter". It is a small platform that carries food from the kitchen to the other rooms in the tower. Find some clues to help you decide which button to press, then jump inside.

4 mousetraps

7 moths

8 cups

21 caterpillars

6 puppies

4 bars of soap

4 wasps

23

The Spellroom

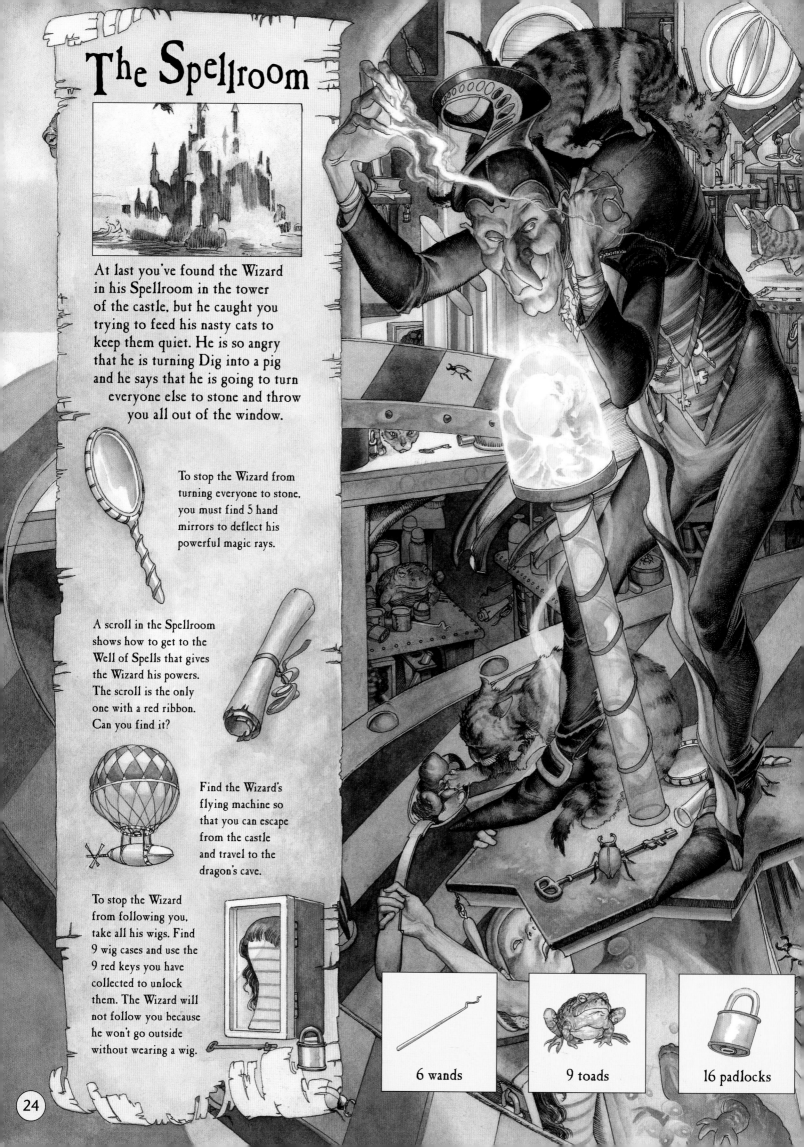

At last you've found the Wizard in his Spellroom in the tower of the castle, but he caught you trying to feed his nasty cats to keep them quiet. He is so angry that he is turning Dig into a pig and he says that he is going to turn everyone else to stone and throw you all out of the window.

To stop the Wizard from turning everyone to stone, you must find 5 hand mirrors to deflect his powerful magic rays.

A scroll in the Spellroom shows how to get to the Well of Spells that gives the Wizard his powers. The scroll is the only one with a red ribbon. Can you find it?

Find the Wizard's flying machine so that you can escape from the castle and travel to the dragon's cave.

To stop the Wizard from following you, take all his wigs. Find 9 wig cases and use the 9 red keys you have collected to unlock them. The Wizard will not follow you because he won't go outside without wearing a wig.

6 wands

9 toads

16 padlocks

18 beetles

6 brushes

10 cats

7 hourglasses

Dragon's Cave

You've finally reached the dragon's cave, deep inside an old gold mine. Winston discovered it years ago while digging for gold. He found that if he kept drinking the water from the Well of Spells it turned him into a great wizard. Now's your chance to defeat the huge dragon, destroy the well and then make your escape.

Your swords are useless against the dragon's scaly skin. Find the pump handle and the hose to pump water from the well into the dragon's mouth. If you put out his fire he won't be able to fight, and will run away.

The railway track leads back to the entrance of the mine which is near Shortsville. The wagon is powered by a small motor. Find 6 lamps and pour the fuel from them into the motor to get it working so that you can escape.

Find 7 sticks of dynamite and the detonator to blow up the cave. When you have done this, the well will be destroyed, the spell will be lifted, everyone's hair will grow again and Dig will return to normal.

7 pickaxes

12 fossils

16 lizards

6 buckets

4 lances

5 helmets

5 shovels

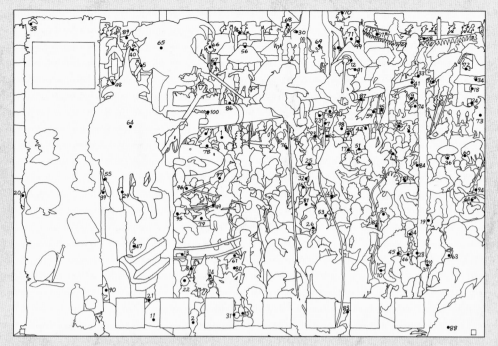

Shortsville 6-7

Sprag 1

Dig 2

Pug 3

Book of maps 4

Swords 5 6 7 8

Axes 9 10

Shields 11 12

Bottles of yab's milk 13 14 15
16 17 18 19

Big bug burgers 20 21 22
23 24 25 26 27 28

Tasty tarts 29 30 31 32 33
34 35 36 37

Snails 38 39 40 41 42 43
44 45 46 47

Ice cream cones 48 49 50
51 52 53 54

Buckets 55 56 57 58 59 60
61 62 63

Judges 64 65 66 67 68 69
70 71 72 73 74 75 76 77
78 79 80 81 82 83 84 85

Yabs 86 87 88

Puppets 89 90 91 92 93 94

Boxing gloves 95 96 97
98 99

Red key 100

Misery Wood 8-9

Doors 1 2 3 4 5 6

Trogs 7 8 9 10 11 12 13 14
15 16 17 18

Rabbits 19 20 21 22 23 24
25 26 27 28 29 30 31 32
33 34 35 36 37 38 39 40
41 42 43 44 45 46 47 48
49 50 51 52

Apples 53 54 55 56 57 58
59 60 61

Mushrooms 62 63 64 65 66
67 68 69 70 71

Birds 72 73 74 75 76 77 78
79 80

Worms 81 82 83 84 85
86 87

Moles 88 89 90 91 92

Clubs 93 94 95 96 97
98 99

Squirrels 100 101 102 103
104 105 106

Flowers 107 108 109 110
111 112 113 114 115 116 117
118 119 120 121 122

Owls 123 124 125 126 127

Butterflies 128 129 130 131
132 133 134 135

Red key 136

The door that leads
to safety is door 5

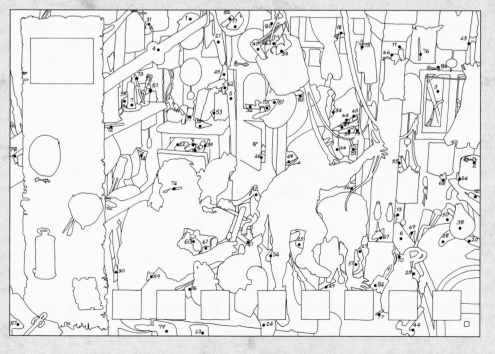

Woodsman's Hut 10-11

Clock 1

Magic key 2

Boat 3

Oars 4 5

Lantern 6

Candles 7 8 9 10 11 12 13

Cheeses 14 15 16 17 18
19 20

Socks 21 22 23 24 25 26
27 28 29

Ducks 30 31 32 33 34 35
36 37 38

Hammers 39 40 41 42
43 44

Saws 45 46 47 48 49 50

Matchboxes 51 52 53 54
55 56

Mice 57 58 59 60 61 62 63
64 65 66 67 68 69 70 71

Pencils 72 73 74 75 76 77

Paintbrushes 78 79 80 81
82 83 84

Red key 85

Stinky Swamp 12–13

Batteries 1 2 3

Spark plugs 4 5

Plug 6

Gold coins 7 8 9 10 11 12
13 14 15 16 17 18

Cherries 19 20 21 22 23
24 25 26

Tadpoles 27 28 29 30
31 32

Herons 33 34 35 36 37 38
39 40

Otters 41 42 43 44 45 46
47 48

Grubs 49 50 51 52 53 54
55 56 57

Piranhas 58 59 60 61 62
63 64 65 66

Skulls 67 68 69 70 71

Snakes 73 74 75 76 77 78
79 80 81

Terrapins 82 83 84 85 86
87 88 89 90 91

Red key 92

Sailor's Rest 14–15

Captain Mullet 1

Anchor and serpent
symbols 2 3 4 5 6 7 8

Wheel 9

Compass 10

Telescope 11

Flag 12

Parakeet pies 13 14 15 16
17 18 19 20

Berry juice 21 22 23 24 25
26 27 28

Eyepatches 29 30 31 32
33 34 35 36 37 38

Parrots 39 40 41 42 43 44
45 46 47 48

Hooks 49 50 51 52 53 54
55 56

Wooden legs 57 58 59
60 61

Watches 62 63 64 65
66 67

Cutlasses 68 69 70 71 72
73 74 75 76

Treasure maps 77 78 79
80 81

Playing cards 82 83 84 85
86 87 88 89 90 91 92
93 94 95 96 97 98 99
100 101 102 103 104

Red key 105

The Serpent 16–17

Helmets 1 2 3 4

Oxygen tanks 5 6 7 8

Boots 9 10 11 12 13 14
15 16

Plug 17

Harpoons 18 19
20 21

Bananas 22 23 24 25
26 27 28 29 30 31
32 33

Crackers 34 35 36 37
38 39 40 41 42 43
44 45

Anchors 46 47 48 49
50 51

Pigs 52 53 54 55 56
57 58 59 60 61

Lobster pots 62 63 64
65 66

Cannon balls 67 68
69 70 71 72 73 74
75 76

Chickens 77 78 79
80 81 82 83 84 85
86 87

Fishing reels 88 89 90
91 92 93 94

Barrels 95 96 97 98
99 100 101

Red key 102

Octopus Ocean 18–19

Submarine 1

Propeller 2

Sewer pipe clues 3 4

Correct pipe 5

Pearls 6 7 8 9 10 11 12 13

Crabs 14 15 16 17 18 19

Octopuses 20 21 22 23 24 25 26 27

Clownfish 28 29 30 31 32 33 34 35 36 37 38 39 40 41 42 43 44 45 46

Eels 47 48 49 50 51 52

Sea urchins 53 54 55 56 57 58 59 60 61 62 63 64

Sharks 65 66 67 68 69 70 71 72

Seahorses 73 74 75 76 77 78 79 80 81 82 83

Starfish 84 85 86 87 88 89 90 91 92 93

Giant clams 94 95 96 97 98

Red key 99

Smelly Sewers 20–21

Correct tunnel 1

Wooden clips 2 3 4 5

Carrot birds 6 7 8 9

Jugs of milk 10 11

Sugar cubes 12 13 14 15 16 17 18 19 20 21 22 23 24

Spoons 25 26 27 28 29 30 31 32

Apple cores 33 34 35 36 37 38 39 40 41 42 43 44 45

Bats 46 47 48 49 50 51 52 53 54 55 56 57

Bones 58 59 60 61 62 63 64 65 66 67 68

Teabags 69 70 71 72 73 74 75 76 77 78 79 80 81 82 83

Rotten eggs 84 85 86 87 88 89 90 91 92 93 94 95 96 97 98

Tin cans 99 100 101 102 103 104 105 106 107 108 109

Banana skins 110 111 112 113 114 115 116 117 118 119 120 121 122 123 124 125 126 127 128

Red key 129

Giant's Kitchen 22–23

Butter 1

Bottle of yab's milk 2

Eggs 3 4 5 6 7 8

Mushrooms 9 10 11 12 13 14 15 16 17

Can opener 18

Cans of cat food 19 20 21 22 23 24 25 26

Tomatoes 27 28 29 30 31 32 33

Slices of bacon 34 35 36 37 38 39 40

Correct button 41 (It's dirty because giant presses it to send food up to tower, and middle bell that wizard rings has no cobwebs on it.)

Wasps 42 43 44 45

Soap 46 47 48 49

Puppies 50 51 52 53 54 55

Caterpillars 56 57 58 59 60 61 62 63 64 65 66 67 68 69 70 71 72 73 74 75 76

Cups 77 78 79 80 81 82 83 84

Moths 85 86 87 88 89 90 91

Mousetraps 92 93 94 95

Red key 96

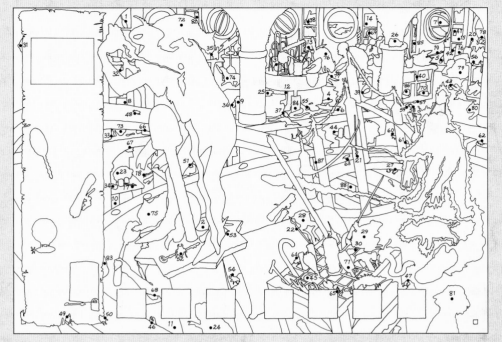

The Spellroom 24–25

Mirrors 1 2 3 4 5	Hourglasses 82 83 84 85
	86 87 88
Scroll with red ribbon 6	
Flying machine 7	
Wig cases 8 9 10 11 12 13	
14 15 16	
Wands 17 18 19 20 21 22	
Toads 23 24 25 26 27 28	
29 30 31	
Padlocks 32 33 34 35 36	
37 38 39 40 41 42 43	
44 45 46 47	
Beetles 48 49 50 51 52 53	
54 55 56 57 58 59 60	
61 62 63 64 65	
Brushes 66 67 68 69	
70 71	
Cats 72 73 74 75 76 77	
78 79 80 81	

Dragon's Cave 26–27

Pump handle 1	Helmets 67 68 69 70 71
Hose 2	
Lamps 3 4 5 6 7 8	
Detonator 9	
Sticks of dynamite 10 11 12	
13 14 15 16	
Pickaxes 17 18 19 20 21	
22 23	
Fossils 24 25 26 27 28 29	
30 31 32 33 34 35	
Lizards 36 37 38 39 40 41	
42 43 44 45 46 47 48	
49 50 51	
Buckets 52 53 54 55	
56 57	
Lances 58 59 60 61	
Shovels 62 63 64 65 66	

Extra puzzles

1. GRANDOS is an anagram – if you rearrange the letters it makes another word. What is it?

2. The Land of Grandos, shown on the map on page 4, is the shape of one of the creatures in this book. Can you see which one?

(Answers are upside down at the bottom of this page.)

Can you find?

~ a bird's nest and a ginger cat in Shortsville?

~ a parachuting mole in Misery Wood?

~ a small photograph in the Woodsman's Hut?

~ a waterskiing terrapin in the Stinky Swamp?

~ an eyeball in the Sailor's Rest?

~ three mice in a lifeboat in *The Serpent*?

~ a clownfish with a hat and a parrot with a snorkel in Octopus Ocean?

~ two rats with hats in the Stinky Sewers?

~ a sleeping bat in the Giant's Kitchen?

~ two snakes and two fish in the Spellroom?

~ a sunbathing lizard in the Dragon's Cave?

Goodbye!

KING ARTHUR'S
KNIGHT
QUEST

Illustrated by
Simone Boni

MISSING

Have you seen these knights?

Sir Lomvert   Sir Swinage   Sir Aquatane

Sir Gawain   Sir Tripont   Sir Larbre

Sir Nocturne   Sir Heronbow   Sir Galahad

Last seen leaving Camelot Castle on various quests.
It is believed that they have had evil spells cast upon
them by Morgan le Fay and are now in mortal danger.

REWARD FOR THEIR SAFE RETURN

King Arthur,

I have kidnapped your knights and I'll never return them.

Ha, ha, ha

Morgan le Fay

GRAND TOURNAMENT

Tuesday, 12 noon on
Camelot Field

(Games in Great Hall if wet)

Win yourself the opportunity to rescue the Knights of the
Round Table by entering the Grand Tournament.

Three lucky winners will get the chance to go on a quest
to save the knights and defeat Morgan le Fay, the wicked
sorceress thought to be responsible for their disappearance.
Anyone who completes the quest successfully will be
made a Knight of the Round Table.

Do you have the courage, wisdom and
strength to be one of the chosen few?

By order of:
Arthur Pendragon,
King of Logres

Information for knight rescuers

Thank you for volunteering to rescue King Arthur's knights and welcome to Camelot, the most wonderful castle in the Kingdom of Logres. Before you set off, there are a few things that you need to know, so please study these pages carefully.

What am I doing in Camelot?

You have been offered a chance to go on a quest to rescue the Knights of the Round Table.

Why do they need rescuing?

Because King Arthur's enemy, the powerful sorceress Morgan le Fay, has cast spells on them so that they cannot return to Camelot. The kingdom is in crisis and the sorceress must be stopped before she seizes the throne and declares herself ruler.

Do I have to go by myself?

No. King Arthur has organized a tournament to select the others to go with you. Each knight that you manage to rescue will also join the quest. Together, you should be powerful enough to defeat Morgan le Fay.

Is the quest dangerous?

Yes, but if you succeed, Arthur will make you a Knight of the Round Table – a great privilege.

How will I recognize Morgan le Fay?

She looks like this picture.

What exactly do I have to do?

Win a place on the quest at the tournament, then set out from Camelot and travel to Morgan le Fay's Castle, rescuing knights along the way. In each place you visit, you will see a picture similar to the one below. One knight needs rescuing in each place. The frame around the picture contains all the information you need.

This tells you where you are in the Kingdom of Logres.

When you have left Camelot, you will see *a shield* in each place you visit. It belongs to the missing knight and shows his coat-of-arms. The sorceress has used her magic on the knight in a way that is linked to the coat-of-arms. Look carefully at the shield and it will help you to find the knight.

The *pieces of parchment* tell you what you have to do in each place that you visit. There are puzzles to solve and things to do.

There's *one piece of knight's equipment* (golden weapons, spurs, a breastplate etc.) hidden in each place you visit, including Camelot. This picture shows what to look for. The complete set of equipment is magical. Whoever wears it will be protected from evil when you reach Morgan le Fay's castle.

In each place you go to *a map* shows you where you are in the Kingdom of Logres. The map on the opposite page shows the whole kingdom.

Merlin's crystal ball shows clues to help you solve the puzzles. Merlin is Arthur's wise magician. He can't come with you because he must stay to protect Arthur, but he'll give you his crystal ball and appear in it with a clue when you need help.

There's *a golden chalice* hidden in each of the first nine places you visit, including Camelot. You'll need all of the chalices later when you meet Morgan le Fay, so don't forget to look for them.

The Grand Tournament is about to begin at Camelot. When you have studied the map of the kingdom, turn the page to find out who will be going with you to rescue King Arthur's Knights...

THE KINGDOM OF LOGRES

Castle le Fay

Fool's Lake

Druid Stones

Green Chapel

Swine Hill

Demon's Bridge

Raven's Wood

Dark Mountains

Pendragon Beacon

Camelot Castle

The Camelot Tournament

Welcome to the tournament to find the people to rescue King Arthur's knights.

The winners will be those who can find a red handkerchief hidden among the trees and present it to the king. Three have already been found. You must find the fourth before anyone else can, and spot which contestants have the other three.

Merlin has a gift that will help you to overcome Morgan le Fay's evil magic. It is a crystal ball that allows you to see Merlin (though not hear him). To prove you are worthy to use it, you must find Merlin and the crystal ball then solve this riddle:

"What can you feel but cannot touch?
What can whistle but has no lips?
What can move trees but cannot be seen?"

Raven's Wood

The first place you visit on your quest is Raven's Wood. Deep in the woods you are attacked by ravens. They think you have come to steal their eggs, which have fallen out of their nests.

To calm the ravens, find seven eggs and an empty nest to put them in.

Hal Hirsuit

Lady Lionheart

There are two mushrooms growing in the woods, one good and one bad. If you feed the knight the good mushroom, he will be freed from Morgan le Fay's spell. If you feed him the other, he will remain a prisoner of the woods forever.

With Merlin's help, find the good mushroom. Then find the missing knight and feed it to him.

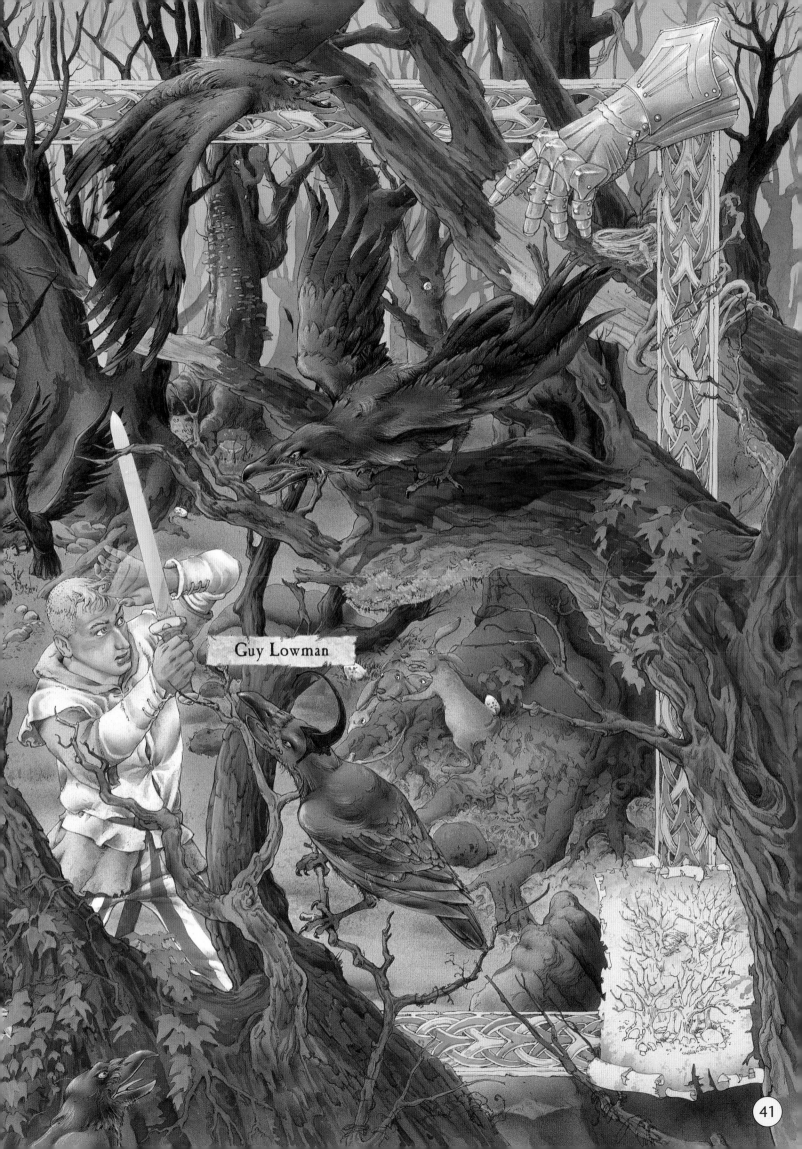

Guy Lowman

Swine Hill

Beyond the woods, on top of a hill, you reach a settlement of pig farmers. They are suspicious of strangers and start to attack you with stones. To show them that you mean no harm, you must find the sacred pig stone and kiss it.

You can identify the bewitched knight by the mark on his body which is different from any other you can see. To free him from the spell, you must find the magic bronze nose ring and place it in his nostrils. Take care – there are many rings in Swine Hill. If you choose the wrong one, the knight will eat pig food for the rest of his days.

Demon's Bridge

Your route is blocked by a fast flowing river, so you must use the Demon's Bridge. Each knight on the bridge guards a different path. One is a powerful warrior from whom it would be impossible to escape. The other is made of stone and is harmless. Find out which is which and cross safely.

Now find Arthur's missing knight and raise him safely to the level of the bridge, using the winch. To operate the winch, first you need to find the winch handle.

You can unlock the knight's cage by turning the correct fish key in the mouth of the fish. Be careful – if you choose the wrong key the knight will fall to his death on the rocks or into the icy water.

The Green Knight

You've reached the Green Knight's Chapel, where the Green Knight challenges you to exchange weapon blows with him. He has the power to replace his head after it has been cut off.

Demand to strike the first blow and then hide his head under the serpent's tail before he can replace it.

The missing knight has been beheaded, but all is not lost. There is a magic belt hidden in the chapel. Find the knight's head and body, place the head on his shoulders and wrap the belt around his neck. The knight will come back to life.

Beware! There are two magic belts. Only the Evergreen Belt will give life, the other kills all that touches it.

Fool's Lake

At Fool's Lake you are taken prisoner by a colony of jesters and clowns. Their leader demands that you roll the dice of death. There are three dice to choose from. You will only be allowed to go if you choose the correct one. By looking carefully at the leader's scroll, you should be able to find out which it is.

King Arthur's knight has been turned into a clown. Many of the clowns carry sticks with models of their own heads on top. Study all the sticks carefully and you should be able to tell which of the clowns is really the knight.

The knight can only be released from the spell through the power of his own tears. When you have found him, you need to find a way of making him cry to break the spell.

The Ferryman

Your next mission is to rescue a knight who is chained to a tree on an island in the middle of the lake. The ferryman will take you there if you solve his riddle: "My bear wants to eat my wolf and my wolf wants to eat my hens. How can I get all my animals safely across to the island, if I can take either the bear or the wolf or the hens in my boat on each crossing?"

The knight's chains are secured with an unbreakable lock.
The Lady of the Lake holds two keys. Only one will open
the lock and free the knight.

If you touch the wrong key, the ferry and everyone aboard
it will be sucked down to the bottom of the lake. If you
choose the correct key, you will be allowed to cross safely
to free the knight from his chains.

Dragon's Cave

An opening in the side of the hill on the island has led you to a cave where a huge dragon lies asleep. If you disturb it, it will eat you and spit out your bones.

The dragon is blocking the main path, so you must find another way across the stones. Don't step on any with bones on them. If you rattle one, you'll wake the dragon.

The knight is imprisoned in one of the towers. You can't call to him or you'll wake the dragon, and you can't see inside the towers. Two towers are open. Inside one is the key to the knight's prison. With Merlin's help, find which tower contains the key and choose a path to reach it. Then find out which tower the knight is in and select a safe route to get to it. If you go into the wrong tower, the door will slam shut and you will be prisoners forever. Once you have rescued the knight, you must find a route out of the dragon's cave.

Monstrous Moat

Beneath the castle of Morgan le Fay, you are attacked by the beast of the moat and the creatures that guard the bridge. The beast is afraid of fire, so it doesn't attack the guards in their flaming turrets.

On the pole of each turret is a lever that lowers the roofs to put out the flames. Find and pull as many levers as you can. The beast will then eat the guards and you can reach the castle.

The knight has been turned into a heron. There are a few
of these birds around the moat, so you will need your wits
about you to find the right one.

To release the knight from his feathery fate, first catch the
fish that glows and feed it to him. You cannot touch the fish
or its power will vanish, so you must find
something to catch it with.

The Sorceress

Inside her castle, Morgan le Fay is about to sacrifice Sir Galahad in a fire that rages from under the Earth. You're losing the battle against her guards, so you must find the magic golden sword that completes the knight's equipment. When your companion has the sword, he'll be able to destroy the guards and stop them from throwing Sir Galahad into the flames.

The nine chalices you have collected on your journey have become scattered around the vaults, along with one other. Recover them all and place the chalice shown on Sir Galahad's shield in one of the eight shrines below the sorceress. If you choose the wrong shrine, the sorceress will destroy you in the fire and the kingdom will be doomed. If you choose correctly, Morgan le Fay will be consumed in her own evil fire and the kingdom will be saved.

The Round Table

Congratulations! You have saved all of King Arthur's knights and rid the kingdom of the evil Morgan le Fay.

The king has set places for the nine knights and for you and your three companions at the Round Table. Can you find out who sits where?

Merlin has discovered a marble stone magically floating in the river. Stuck into the stone is a fabulous sword with this inscription on its blade: "Whoever solves my riddle can withdraw me and sit at the king's left side: 'Find a beast in a circle of light. The living beast wears a symbol. The woven symbol hides my twin. Excalibur is its name. Return it to the king.'" When you have found Excalibur, you can draw the sword from the stone. King Arthur can knight you and your companions and you can take your place by his side as a Knight of the Round Table.

The Camelot Tournament 38–39

Golden shield 1

Chalice 2

Red handkerchiefs 3 4 5 6

Merlin and the crystal ball 7

Riddle answer: the wind

Raven's Wood 40–41

Golden gauntlet 1

Chalice 2

Missing knight: Sir Lomvert 3

Nest 4

Eggs 5 6 7 8 9 10 11

Good mushroom 12

Bad mushroom 13

Swine Hill 42–43

Golden helmet 1

Chalice 2

Missing knight: Sir Swinage 3

Pig stone 4

Nose ring 5

Demon's Bridge 44-45

Golden breastplate 1

Chalice 2

Missing knight:
Sir Aquatane 3

Living warrior 4

Stone warrior 5

Winch handle 6

Fish key 7

The Green Knight 46-47

Golden spur 1

Chalice 2

Missing knight:
Sir Gawain's body 3,
Sir Gawain's head 3A

Serpent's tail 4

Evergreen Belt 5

Wrong belt 6

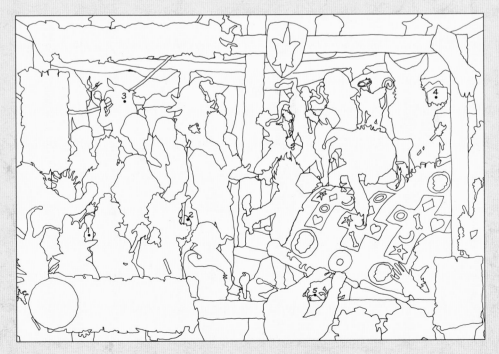

Fool's Lake 48-49

Golden gauntlet 1

Chalice 2

Missing knight:
Sir Tripont 3
(his clown stick is
a knight's helmet)

Correct die 4

Onion 5
(to make the knight cry)

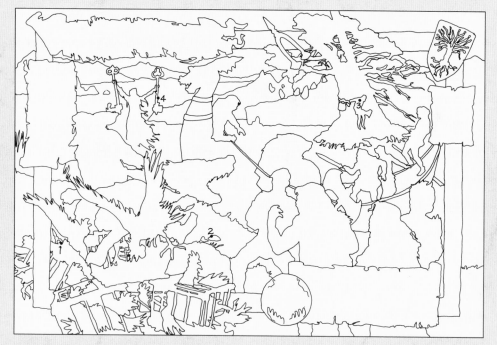

The Ferryman 50–51

Golden spur 1

Chalice 2

Missing knight: Sir Larbre 3

Correct key 4

Riddle answer:

Step 1. Take the wolf across to the island and row back.

Step 2. Take the hens across to the island and bring the wolf back.

Step 3. Leave the wolf on the mainland and take the bear across to the island.

Step 4. Take the wolf across to the island.

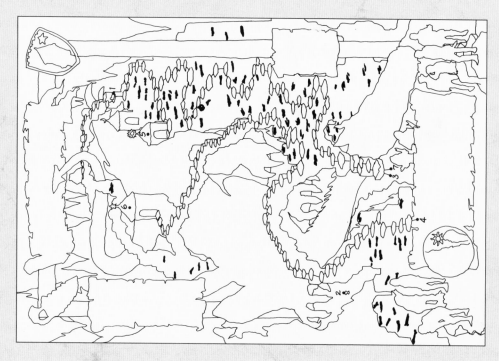

Dragon's Cave 52–53

Golden shoe 1

Chalice 2

Route to key tower 3

Missing knight: Sir Nocturne. Route to his tower 4

Key tower 5

Sir Nocturne's tower 6

Route out of cave 7

Monstrous Moat 54–55

Golden shoe 1

Chalice 2

Missing knight: Sir Heronbow 3

Levers 4 5 6 7 8

Glowing fish 9

Net 10

The Sorceress 56–57

Golden sword 1

Chalices 2 3 4
5 6 7 8 9 10

Sir Galahad's chalice 11

Correct shrine 12

The Round Table 58–59

Sir Lomvert 1 Chair C1	Sir Galahad 9 Chair C9
Sir Swinage 2 Chair C2	Lady Lionheart 10 Chair C10
Sir Aquatane 3 Chair C3	Hal Hirsuit 11 Chair C11
Sir Gawain 4 Chair C4	Guy Lowman 12 Chair C12
Sir Tripont 5 Chair C5	Beast in a circle of light 13
Sir Larbre 6 Chair C6	Living beast 14
Sir Nocturne 7 Chair C7	Woven symbol 15
Sir Heronbow 8 Chair C8	Excalibur 16
	Reader's chair 17

Did you also see these strange sights?

~ a lizard with six legs in Raven's Wood?

~ a man with a saucepan on his head at Swine Hill?

~ a monkey with wings on Fool's Lake?

~ a skull at the Demon's Bridge?

~ a ram's head in the Chapel of the Green Knight?

~ the ferryman's bad foot?

~ a lucky duck who escaped the cooking pot at the Round Table?

Thank you!

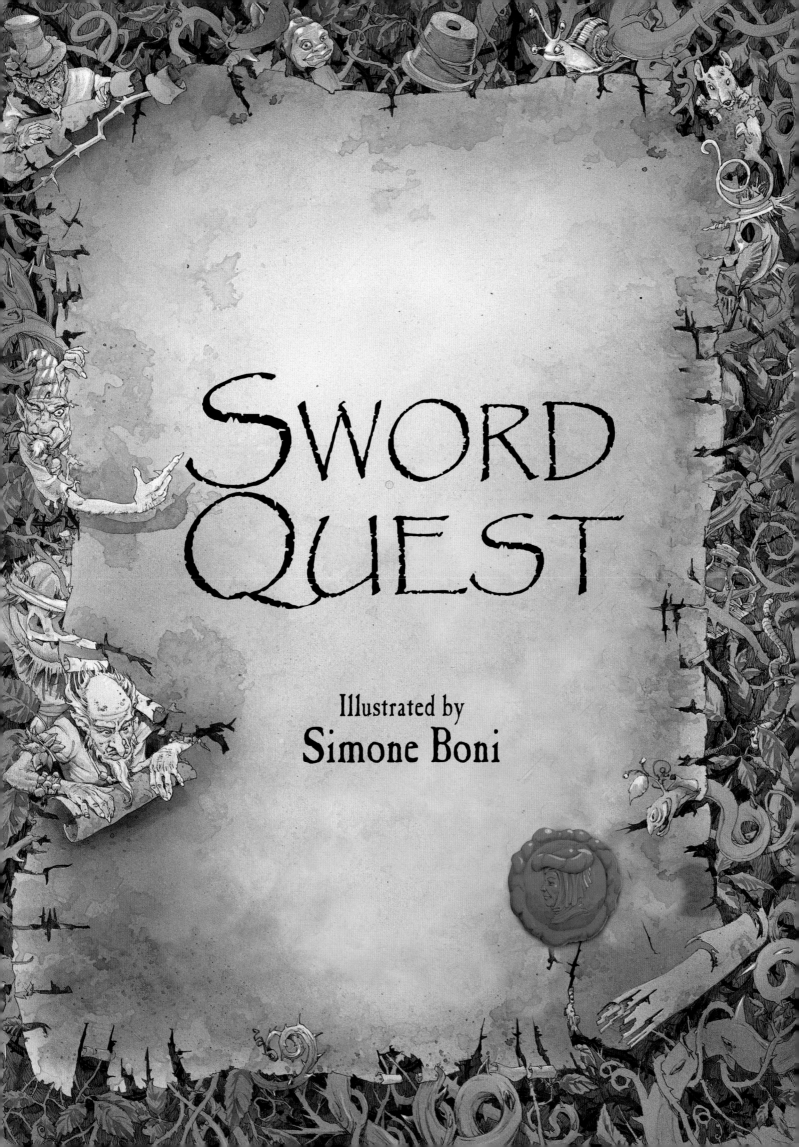

Sword Quest

Illustrated by

Simone Boni

Good Citizens of Gladlands,

I bring you bad tidings of great woe. A terrible calamity has befallen our kingdom – the sacred Sword of Glee has been taken from us; stolen by the evil, shape-changing villain, Blag the Untrustworthy! Disguised as our good king, Blag crept into Castle Glee and tricked Muddle the Magician, the keeper of the sword, into handing it over. But that nasty creature Blag did not stop there. Using the sword's great power for his own evil ends, he kidnapped the real king, Gilbert the Gracious, and now holds him prisoner in Castle Gloom on the far side of Gladlands.

I have just received a ransom note from Blag demanding that we all go to work as his slaves in the Fields of Fancy, growing crops for his armies so that they may grow ever stronger. If we do not submit to his evil plan, we will never see Gilbert again!

The time has come to put a stop to Blag's wicked ways. I call upon all Gladlanders to compete in a tournament at Castle Glee to find the bravest, strongest and wisest amongst us to defeat Blag, and return the king and the sword to their rightful home. So, good citizens, I am looking for:

VOLUNTEERS TO GO ON THE SWORD QUEST

Will you be one of the chosen few? Come to the tournament and find out.

By order of

Gladys the Glamorous

(The king's grandmother)

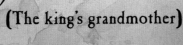

Important information for all questers

Thank you for volunteering to go on the Sword Quest, and welcome to Gladlands. There are some things you need to know before you set off.

Where am I?

You are at Castle Glee in Gladlands where a terrible calamity has struck the royal family.

Oh dear! What happened?

An evil, shape-changing villain, named Blag the Untrustworthy, has kidnapped Gilbert the Gracious, Gladland's rightful ruler, and is holding him prisoner in Castle Gloom. Blag has also stolen the sacred Sword of Glee which is the source of all Gilbert's power.

Oh no! Anything else I should know?

Yes indeed. Blag has sent Gilbert's granny, Gladys the Glamorous, a ransom note, demanding that all Gladlanders work as his slaves in the Fields of Fancy. If they refuse they will never see Gilbert again.

So what can I do about it?

Go on the quest to Castle Gloom to rescue King Gilbert, defeat Blag the Untrustworthy and bring the magic sword and the king back to Castle Glee.

Who'll go with me?

Gladys has organized a grand tournament at Castle Glee. The three winners will go with you on the Sword Quest. The tournament is starting soon.

How much time do we have?

Not long. Every day that Blag has the magic sword his evil powers grow stronger. Your mission must be accomplished as quickly as possible.

How do we get to Castle Gloom?

You'll set out from Castle Glee and travel through Gladlands. The map below shows the whole of Gladlands. Please study it carefully.

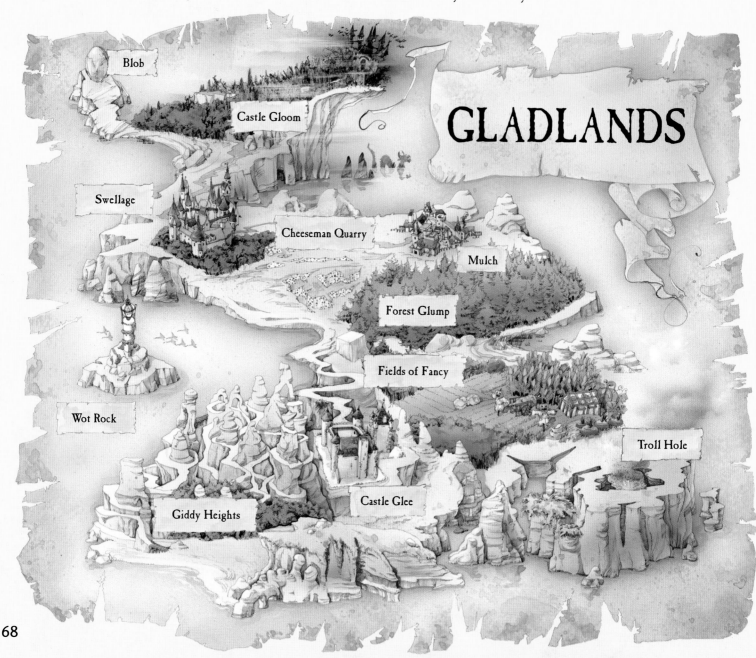

Blob

Castle Gloom

GLADLANDS

Swellage

Cheeseman Quarry

Mulch

Forest Glump

Fields of Fancy

Wot Rock

Troll Hole

Giddy Heights

Castle Glee

The parchments

The quest will be both difficult and dangerous, so you will need courage, cunning and the eyes of an eagle if you are to survive. In every place you visit you will see a piece of parchment similar to the one below. It contains vital information to get you safely through to the next stage of the quest.

Magic Boat

SAMPLE

The boat is a magical place. It is small on the outside but enormous inside, and it's full of toys that the old sailor collected on his travels around the world. He also used it as a workshop to create wonderful new toys. You must find out how the boat works before you can continue your journey.

Somewhere there is a clockwork sailor who steers the boat. He will only work when he is wearing his sailor's hat and is wound up with a special key. If you can find the sailor, the hat and the key, you can begin your boat trip.

There are some model castles on the boat. To make the clockwork sailor steer the boat in the right direction, find the model that looks like Castle Gloom (before Blag let it go to wrack and ruin) and place it in the direction finder.

In the engine room, on the lower deck, a clockwork man stokes the furnace with coal. To get the boat moving you need to find 7 lumps of coal for him.

There are many pies in the boat, but only four of them are real. The others are toys. Find 4 real pies.

This tells you where you are in Gladlands.

These maps will help to remind you where each place is in Gladlands. They come from a collection of maps owned by Muddle the Magician of Castle Glee.

When it is time, read these pieces of information carefully. They contain some very important clues.

The pictures show people or things you have to find or avoid in each place you visit. Some will be very hard to spot, because you can only see a small part of them.

Some pictures show things you will need later in the quest or ways of getting to the next place.

At the bottom of the parchment are pictures of food or drink to look for. You can find something to eat in each place you visit.

The squares

At the bottom of each page are some more pictures in squares. The numbers tell you how many of that thing you can spot in the main scene. Finding these things will sharpen your skills and help you to survive the quest.

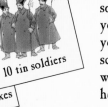

5 jack-in-the-boxes

10 tin soldiers

Your enemy, Blag the Untrustworthy, holding the sacred Sword of Glee.

You can recognize Blag from his one white eye, which he cannot change.

Blag's eye

Blag the Untrustworthy is a master of disguise and can change himself into anything he wants to be, but one thing always gives him away: he has one white eye which he cannot change. Keep a lookout for him in each place you visit, because he may be hiding, getting ready to trick you.

The gemstones

Hidden in each of the first ten places you visit is one gemstone. You will need all ten later to help you defeat Blag, so don't forget to look for them.

The Castle Glee tournament is about to begin. Turn the page to find out who will be going with you on the SWORD QUEST...

Castle Glee

Welcome to the Tournament of Knighthood at Castle Glee. Gladys the Glamorous is busy looking for the three people with enough courage, cunning and skill to go with you on the quest to retrieve the Sword of Glee. Can you find the ones she's chosen in the crowd?

Sir Loin du Stake is an elderly knight with a rusty sword and shield. He wears a monocle in his right eye.

Lady Egg wears an orange three pointed hat. She has a beauty spot above her lip.

Tern the Page wears one green shoe and one brown shoe, and takes his pet woffit with him wherever he goes.

Castle Gloom is far away. You will need to travel there on quockback. Can you find 4 quocks?

You'll be very hungry after the tournament. Find 20 assorted cakes, and a fish sandwich to eat.

9 woffits

5 drums

7 sticky sticks

7 rattles
4 abacuses
5 goblets
10 red noses
10 stingers

Magic Workshop

You have been called into Muddle the Magician's workshop so that he and Gladys can give you some vital equipment and information for your quest. When you arrive you find that one of Muddle's magic spells has gone wrong. Everything is floating around the room.

First find the butterfly net and catch the Spellbook, so that you can reverse the spell. It will then take a day or so for the magic to wear off. Take the Spellbook with you on your journey.

You will need a map of Gladlands to help you reach Castle Gloom. Find the map holder.

Gladys has brought the ancient weapons of Glee for you to take on your journey. There are 4 sharp swords and 4 shields to find.

Good food and drink is very important on a long journey. Find 12 crabby apples and 6 water bags.

13 potion bottles

6 dividers

7 pestles

5 microscopes

8 quills

17 lizards

6 pairs of spectacles

9 crystal balls

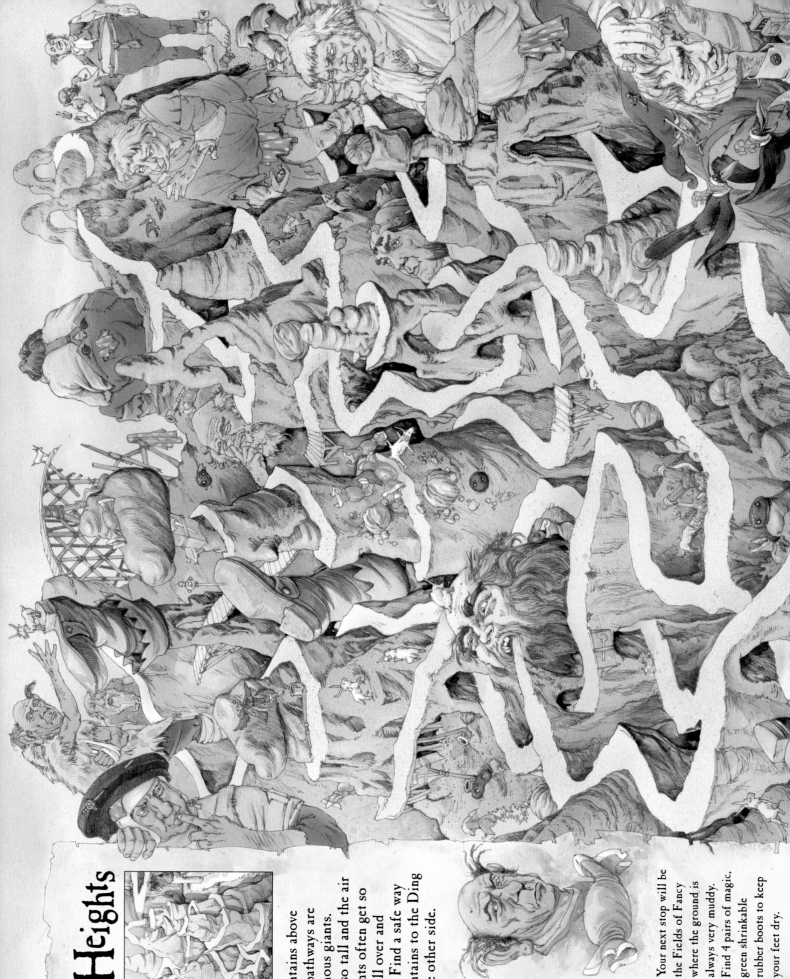

Giddy Heights

High in the mountains above Castle Glee, the pathways are guarded by enormous giants. Because they are so tall and the air is so thin, the giants often get so dizzy that they fall over and damage the paths. Find a safe way through the mountains to the Ding Dong gates on the other side.

To pass the giants safely, give each of them a mint to suck to stop their ears from popping when they stand up. There are 17 giants and 17 mints to find.

Your next stop will be the Fields of Fancy where the ground is always very muddy. Find 4 pairs of magic, green shrinkable rubber boots to keep your feet dry.

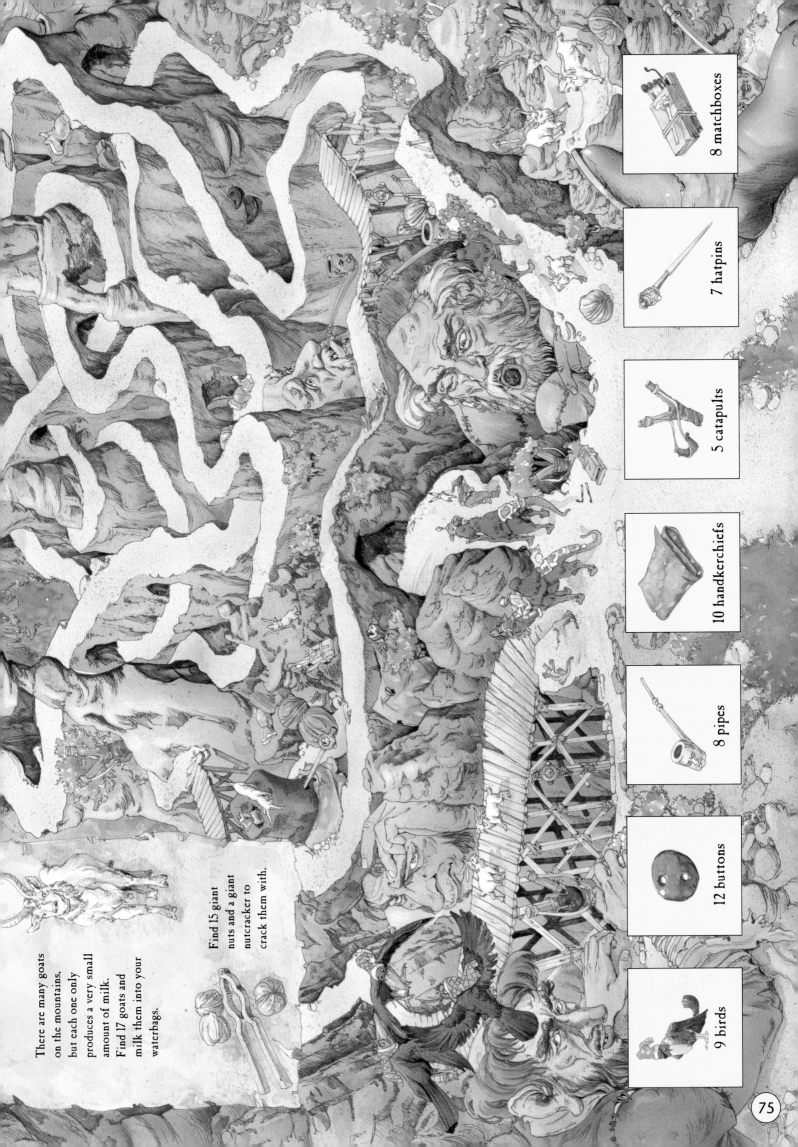

There are many goats on the mountains, but each one only produces a very small amount of milk. Find 17 goats and milk them into your waterbags.

Find 15 giant nuts and a giant nutcracker to crack them with.

8 matchboxes

7 hatpins

5 catapults

10 handkerchiefs

8 pipes

12 buttons

9 birds

Fields of Fancy

In the middle of the Fields of Fancy you are discovered by a group of fleebs. Fleebs are in charge of everyone that works here and they know that you are strangers because of your boots – only townsfolk wear green rubber boots in the country. Now they plan to catch you and bury you in the soil to see if you will grow.

To stop the fleebs, you must lure each one of them to one of the pots on sticks that are used for trapping earwigs. When the fleeb is under a pot, shake the stick and move back quickly. The pot will fall and trap him. There are 8 fleebs and 9 pots on sticks to find.

It is too dangerous to continue through the fields on foot. But if you find 4 worms to feed the giant bird, it may fly you to safety.

The only food that's small enough for you to carry are peas. Find 5 peas and fill your water bags from the watering can.

5 mice

5 hoes

5 jars

8 snails   6 scarecrows   3 spray cans   5 packets of seeds   9 earwigs

Mulch Market

The giant bird has dropped you in the town of Mulch. Every day is market day in Mulch, so it's always full of strange people and weird creatures. It's an extremely dirty, smelly and noisy place to be. You're still a long way from Castle Gloom. You need to find some way of getting there.

If you can get hold of a boat, you can sail all the way to Castle Gloom on the river that runs through Mulch. Sir Loin has found out that there's a sailor in the town who'll give you a boat in return for some glugs. The old man has always dreamed of starting his own glug farm. Find 11 baby glugs and the sailor.

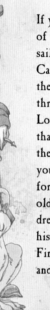

A glug

Some of Blag's soldiers are in town. They have orders to capture any strangers. Spot all eight, so you can avoid them.

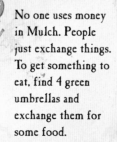

No one uses money in Mulch. People just exchange things. To get something to eat, find 4 green umbrellas and exchange them for some food.

7 clothears

5 quock droppings

7 plants

3 sacks of grain　　8 giant grubs　　11 cluck eggs　　3 wheelbarrows　　9 trunkbills

Magic Boat

The boat is a magical place. It is small on the outside, but enormous inside, and it's full of toys that the old sailor collected on his travels around the world. He also used it as a workshop to create wonderful new toys. You must find out how the boat works before you can continue your journey.

Somewhere there is a clockwork sailor who steers the boat. He will only work when he is wearing his sailor's hat and is wound up with a special key. If you can find the sailor, the hat and the key, you can begin your boat trip.

There are some model castles on the boat. To make the clockwork sailor steer the boat in the right direction, find the model that looks like Castle Gloom (before Blag let it go to wrack and ruin) and place it in the direction finder.

In the engine room, on the lower deck, a clockwork man stokes the furnace with coal. To get the boat moving you need to find 7 lumps of coal for him.

There are many pies in the boat, but only four of them are real. The others are toys. Find 4 real pies.

5 jack-in-the-boxes

3 silly masks

10 tin soldiers

7 hoppers

6 fishmobiles

10 cuddly toys

4 flying machines

7 baby dolls

Swellheads

The boat has drifted into a small town where the Swellheads live. The Swellheads are very clever and have very big heads to make room for their very big brains. They are only interested in things that will improve their knowledge, but they seem fairly friendly.

The Swellheads would like to study your boat, but this will take them a very long time. (It takes them a very long time to do anything.) You don't have time to spare, so you need to exchange your boat for another. Can you find a punt and a pole?

It will soon be dark, so you will need to find something to light your way. Find a lamp and a bottle of lamp fuel.

Swellheads are usually so busy that they forget to eat. You will have to help yourselves to whatever half-eaten food they have left lying around. Find 4 forgotten fruit pies and 5 lost bottles of lemonade.

The Swellheads have mislaid the handle that opens the lock gates on the canal. You have to find the handle to continue your journey.

9 teapots

12 red books

18 monkeys

6 toasting forks   5 clocks   5 stoves   9 teacups   5 brown shoes

The Delves

The river runs through a forest where you are captured by delves. Delves are nasty pointy creatures who steal things from others. They have just stolen your boat and all your weapons, but they will let you go unharmed if you do something to help them.

The delves' machine for carrying water from the river to the treetops is broken. One of the cogs is missing. If you can find the cog, the delves will help you get to Castle Gloom.

There is a blind delve who knows about a secret underground tunnel which leads right to the heart of Castle Gloom. He wears dark glasses and carries a stick like this one. Can you find him?

The blind delve says the entrance to the tunnel is in the side of a hollow tree. Can you spot it?

There is no food in the tunnel. You will need to find 8 roasted cluck legs for the journey.

9 owls

7 stinger nests

11 ladders

8 moths 8 torches 6 concertinas 6 buckets 6 knives

Clown Dungeon

You have been betrayed! The blind delve was really Blag in disguise. He has thrown you into the Clown Dungeon in Castle Gloom, where King Gilbert the Gracious is also being held prisoner. Now you are standing on a rotating platform, surrounded by rows of stone carvings and some very hungry crocodiles.

The platform is turning so fast, you are in danger of being thrown into the crocodile pit. To stop the platform, find the hand on the clown statue that is different in some way, and twist it clockwise.

Now you must find a copy of the clown's face among the row of snake carvings and push its red nose with one of your pointing sticks.

Pointing stick

The platform will then rise to the next level where you must find the clown's face again and push its nose. If you do this quickly on each of the 5 levels, the platform will raise you out of the dungeon. But if you are too slow, it will sink and you will be eaten by the crocodiles.

The crocodiles get fed with fish once a day, but they prefer to eat people. There are lots of spare fish for you to eat if you can catch them with your pointing sticks.

5 forks

14 frogs

11 watches

18 starfish

8 cheeses

5 padlocks

13 skulls

6 loaves

The Great Hall

After escaping from the dungeon, you find yourselves in the Great Hall of Castle Gloom where Blag's personal guard of Grunts are eating. Grunts are the most smelly, filthy creatures in the whole world. Their smell is so bad, no one can stand being near them long enough to defeat them.

Grunts are afraid of only one thing – being clean. If you can find the fire hose and hydrant to spray the Grunts with water, they will run away.

It would take forever to find the sword in Castle Gloom's hundreds of rooms and secret passages. The only way to track it down is to follow Blag. He is disguised as one of the Grunts, but you can recognize him by his one white eye. Find Blag and follow him.

You will need plenty of energy if you are going to defeat Blag. Gather up all the food you can. There are 13 slices of stinky pizza and 4 jugs of jungle juice to find.

7 dominoes

6 plates

9 rats

5 glasses   6 woodworms   6 oil paintings   12 candles   8 shields

The Ramparts

You have followed Blag up to the very top of Castle Gloom. Using the power of the magic sword, he has brought all the stone carvings, called gargoyles, to life. The gargoyles are very nasty. They will bite you and throw you off the top of the castle unless you stop them.

You should have already found 10 magic gemstones on your travels. If you throw one gemstone into each of the gargoyles' mouths, the spell will be broken and they will turn to stone again.

Using the power of the sword, Blag has created a magic ball that protects him from your weapons. The only way to fight magic is with stronger magic. In the Spellbook there is one spell which is powerful enough to defeat Blag. Collect all the ingredients, follow the spell, and Blag will vanish forever.

Of all the spells inside this book, this one deserves a second look. It will destroy all evil powers (especially magic balls on towers). Put *3 red leaves* into a cup, and with *a pencil* mash them up. Collect *5 spiders* from the wall. Into the cup they all must fall. Now take *2 feathers* from a nest and find *the grub that's dressed the best.* Then mix them slowly one and all and throw them at the magic ball.

To be magically transported home, find the clocktower and the key to open its door. Step inside, put your hands on the sword and say this spell:

Hands of time – it's half past three,
And time we went to Castle Glee.
Our quest is done, and we have won,
The king and sword are free!
(Hurrah!)

7 clock springs

8 hammers

3 raverbird eggs

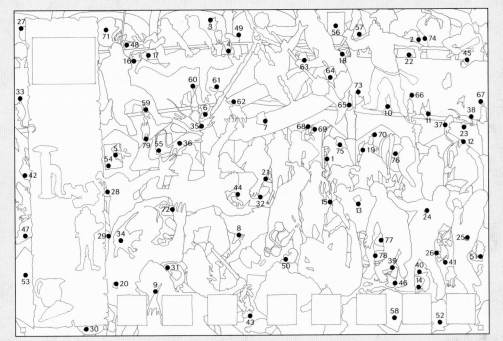

The Great Hall 88–89

Hose and hydrant 1

Blag 2

Slices of pizza 3 4 5 6 7 8 9 10 11 12 13 14 15

Jugs of jungle juice 16 17 18 19

Dominoes 20 21 22 23 24 25 26

Plates 27 28 29 30 31 32

Rats 33 34 35 36 37 38 39 40 41

Glasses 42 43 44 45 46

Woodworms 47 48 49 50 51 52

Oil paintings 53 54 55 56 57 58

Candles 59 60 61 62 63 64 65 66 67 68 69 70

Shields 71 72 73 74 75 76 77 78

Gems 79

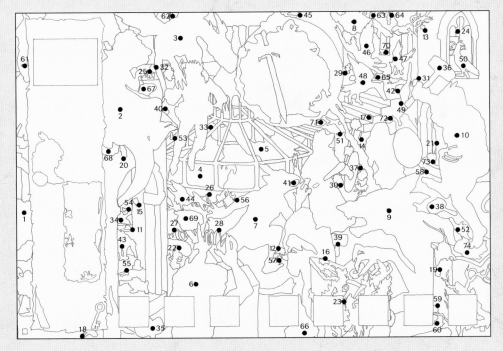

The Ramparts 90–91

Gargoyles 1 2 3 4 5 6 7 8 9 10

Red leaves 11 12 13

Pencil 14

Spiders 15 16 17 18 19

Feathers 20 21

Well-dressed grub 22

Key to clock tower 23

Clock tower 24

Clock springs 25 26 27 28 29 30 31

Hammers 32 33 34 35 36 37 38 39

Raverbird eggs 40 41 42

Raverbirds 43 44 45 46 47 48 49 50 51 52

Bent nails 53 54 55 56 57 58 59 60

Chimneys 61 62 63 64 65 66

Nests 67 68 69 70 71 72 73 74

Did you also notice?

~ five tiny men stealing cakes in Castle Glee?

~ a light bulb in the Magic Workshop?

~ a giant picking his nose in Giddy Heights?

~ a game of snakes and ladders in the Magic Boat?

~ a rat sitting on someone's head in the Great Hall?

~ a miserable earwig and a frightened giant grub in the Dungeon?

~ a toy pie in the Dungeon?

~ a toy pie in the Great Hall?

~ 3 skulls among the Delves?

~ 2 pigs, a lizard and a goat among the Delves?

~ an imprisoned goat in the Dungeon?

~ a crocodile that could be Blag in the Dungeon?

Goodbye!

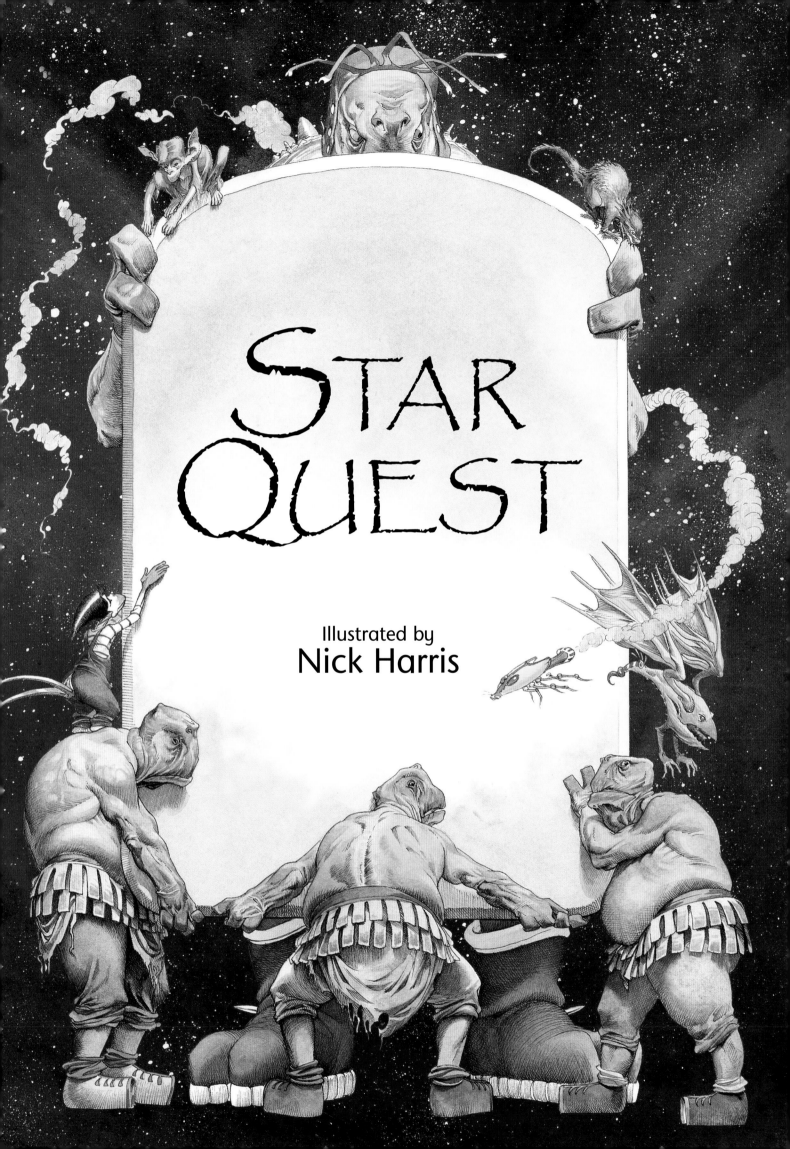

STAR QUEST

Illustrated by
Nick Harris

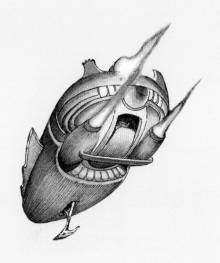

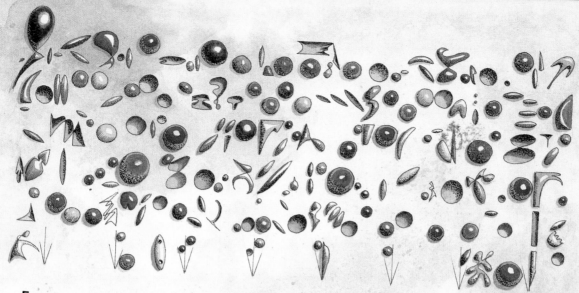

Earthspeak translation:

Greetings Earthlings!

Do not be alarmed. I come in peace.

My name is Plib. I have come from the small planet of Bliss in a galaxy far away. On behalf of the inhabitants of Bliss, I have come to deliver an important message and ask for your help.

Our planet, like your Earth, was once a nice place to live, but it is quickly becoming a frozen wasteland. Evil Lord Glaxx, leader of a group of intergalactic space thugs, named the Lava Louts, has developed a laser beam that can suck all the energy from stars. At this very moment he is draining the star which gives our planet all its heat and light. Without energy we shall all freeze and die in ice and darkness.

Glaxx's plan is to suck all the energy from stars throughout the universe and to destroy life on all planets. He must be stopped! It is only a matter of time before he reaches Earth and sucks the life from your star, the Sun.

If there is anyone on Earth brave and clever enough to help me and my planet, please join me on the greatest adventure of your life...

THE STAR QUEST.

With thanks, Plib

Important information for all questers

Thank you for volunteering to go on the Star Quest, and welcome to Star World – the most exciting leisure park on Planet Earth. Before you set off on the quest there are some things you need to know. Please study this information carefully and look at the picture of Planet Bliss at the bottom of this page.

What's the problem?

Evil Lord Glaxx, leader of the Lava Louts whose bodies are made entirely of molten lava, has developed a powerful laser that extracts the energy from stars. At this very moment he is in the process of draining the energy from a star that provides all the heat and light for a small planet called Bliss.

Why should I care?

It's only a matter of time before Lord Glaxx comes to our galaxy and turns his laser on our own star – the Sun. When he does, the Earth and everything on it will be frozen – forever!

Can Glaxx be stopped?

Only if you can find Plib, the messenger from Bliss, agree to help him track down Lord Glaxx, and put a stop to his evil exploits, can you help save the planet.

Can't someone else help?

There's room for two more Earthlings, as well as you, on board Plib's spaceship. The first two people that walk into the ship will accompany you, if Plib can persuade them to help him.

How soon do we have to go?

Now. Lord Glaxx will soon finish draining the star, leaving Planet Bliss just a freezing, lifeless ball in the depths of space. There's no time to lose.

How do we get there?

You'll set out from Star World in Plib's spacecraft and head for Planet Bliss far, far away.

THE PLANET OF BLISS

Jelly Stones

Blange

Bliss's Star

Ooh Aah Forest

Craterland

Tentacle Towers

Squirm Island

Loch Lung

Mug Swamp

Crystal Desert

Lava Mountains

Ice Lands

Glaxx's Ship

How to do the puzzles

The quest will be difficult and dangerous, so you will need skill, courage and the eyes of an eagle if you are to survive. In each place you visit you will see a panel similar to the one below. It explains what you have to do in that place before you can move on to the next stage of the quest.

Ice Lands

You escape from the space station, but your ship was hit by the station's laser cannons and you are forced to make an emergency landing in Ice Lands on Star World. Before Glaxx started draining energy from the star, most of the planet's crops were grown here. Now it's a frozen wasteland.

Many of Glaxx's soldiers are here playing winter sports. You must find some clothes to keep warm and disguise yourselves. Find 4 pairs of snow boots, 4 pairs of goggles, 4 snow hats and 4 gooth skin coats. Don't take anything that the soldiers are wearing.

Plib's ship is damaged beyond repair and his home is on the other side of the mountains. Plib says there is a tunnel that will take you there. Find the entrance to the tunnel.

The snow is too deep to walk through, but you must reach the tunnel. There is an abandoned snow craft half buried in the snow. Find the snow craft and its handlebars, and also find a shovel to dig them out. Put them together and head for the tunnel.

Find a pot of melted gooth's cheese and 6 crusts of bread to take with you.

This tells you where you are.

These pictures and maps show you where each place is. Plib, the alien, has copies of all of them.

When it is time, read these pieces of information carefully. They contain some very important clues.

The pictures on the panels show creatures or things you have to find or avoid in each place you visit. Some will be very hard to spot, because you can only see a small part of them.

Some pictures show things you will need later in the quest, or ways of getting to the next place.

Somewhere on the panels are pictures of food and drinks to look for. You can find something to eat in nearly every place you visit.

9 two-headed ponguins

now boards

Along the bottom of each page are some more pictures in squares. The numbers tell you how many of that thing you can spot in the main scene. Finding these things will sharpen your skills and help you survive the quest.

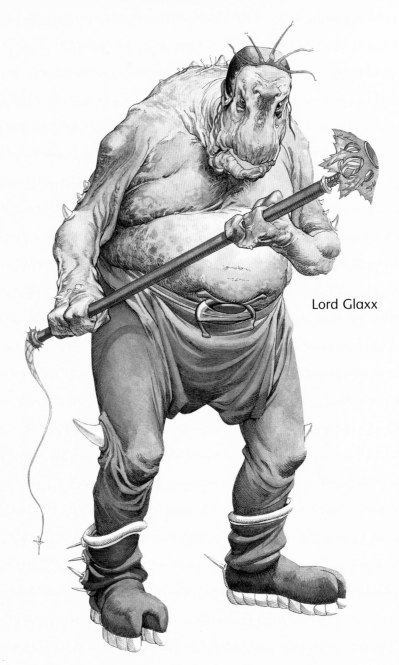

Lord Glaxx

The energy crystals

After you have left Star World, you will need to find one energy crystal in each of the first seven places you visit. In the eighth place there are three crystals. You will need all ten crystals later to help you defeat Glaxx, so don't forget to look for them.

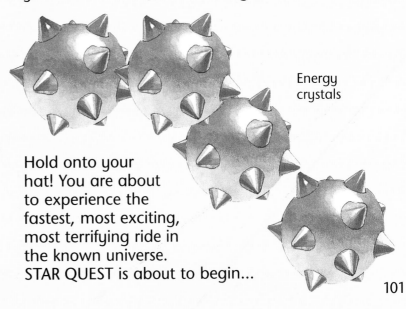

Energy crystals

Hold onto your hat! You are about to experience the fastest, most exciting, most terrifying ride in the known universe. STAR QUEST is about to begin...

Star World

You are at Star World, the biggest space theme park on Earth. You don't have time to go on any of the rides, because you must find Plib, who is the only real alien here. You also need to spot the two people who will be going with you on the Star Quest.

Plib is having trouble convincing anyone that his story is true. Soon he'll have to return to his spaceship. Can you spot him?

Two children, named Jess and Harry, are walking over to Plib's spaceship, thinking it's just another ride. Can you find them?

Jess wears red ribbons in her hair and carries a small, furry backpack in the shape of a dog.

Harry is very tall for his age and has red hair that he can never comb flat.

You won't be able to go anywhere unless you can find Plib's spaceship. Can you see it?

Can you find 5 starburgers and 5 solarshakes to take with you on the long journey?

7 space helmets

9 roadrunners

12 lollipops

14 Star World hats

10 security guards

9 prairie dogs

35 balloons

Plib's Ship

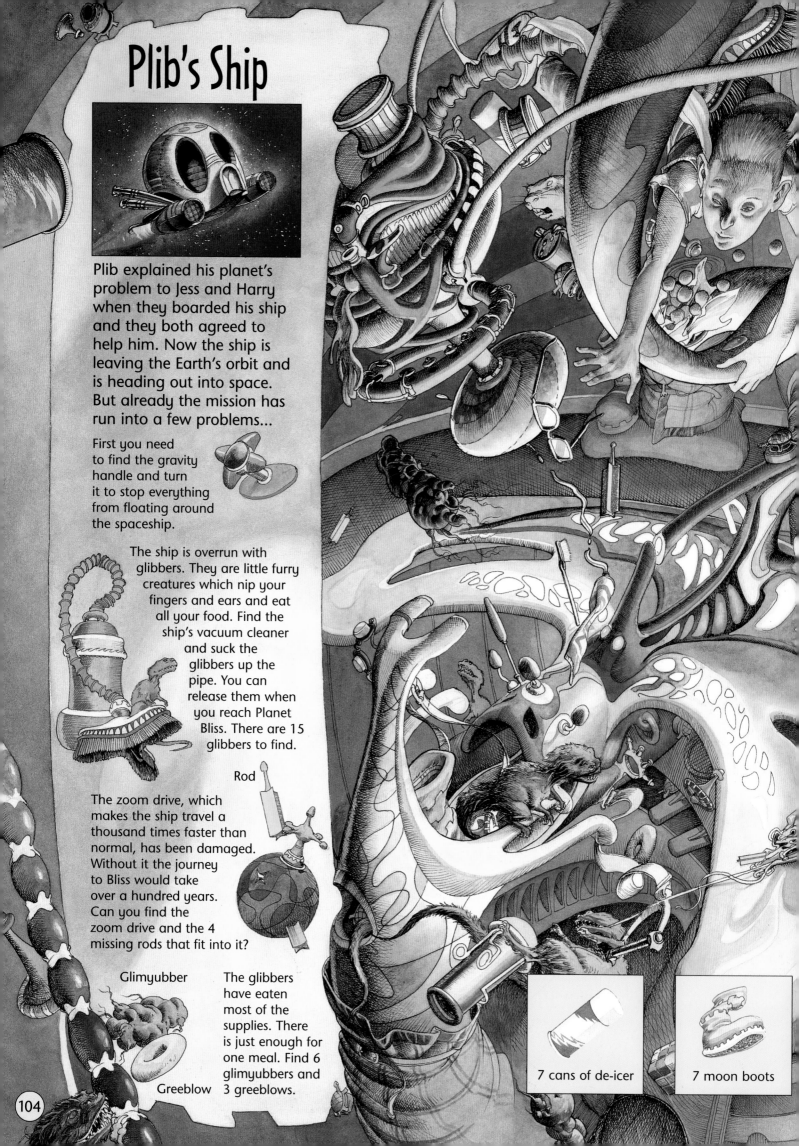

Plib explained his planet's problem to Jess and Harry when they boarded his ship and they both agreed to help him. Now the ship is leaving the Earth's orbit and is heading out into space. But already the mission has run into a few problems...

First you need to find the gravity handle and turn it to stop everything from floating around the spaceship.

The ship is overrun with glibbers. They are little furry creatures which nip your fingers and ears and eat all your food. Find the ship's vacuum cleaner and suck the glibbers up the pipe. You can release them when you reach Planet Bliss. There are 15 glibbers to find.

Rod

The zoom drive, which makes the ship travel a thousand times faster than normal, has been damaged. Without it the journey to Bliss would take over a hundred years. Can you find the zoom drive and the 4 missing rods that fit into it?

Glimyubber

The glibbers have eaten most of the supplies. There is just enough for one meal. Find 6 glimyubbers and 3 greeblows.

Greeblow

7 cans of de-icer

7 moon boots

5 pairs of goggles

14 spare fuses

4 travel blankets

6 music cylinders

17 air fresheners

Space Station

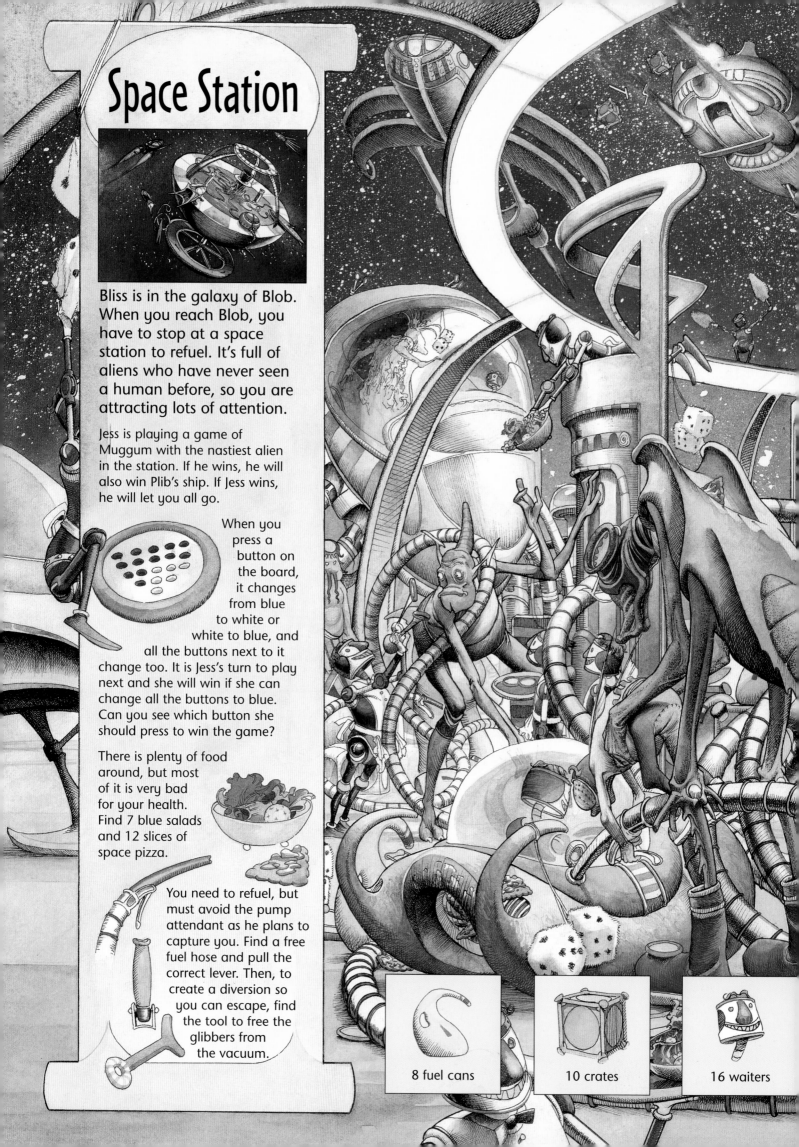

Bliss is in the galaxy of Blob. When you reach Blob, you have to stop at a space station to refuel. It's full of aliens who have never seen a human before, so you are attracting lots of attention.

Jess is playing a game of Muggum with the nastiest alien in the station. If he wins, he will also win Plib's ship. If Jess wins, he will let you all go.

When you press a button on the board, it changes from blue to white or white to blue, and all the buttons next to it change too. It is Jess's turn to play next and she will win if she can change all the buttons to blue. Can you see which button she should press to win the game?

There is plenty of food around, but most of it is very bad for your health. Find 7 blue salads and 12 slices of space pizza.

You need to refuel, but must avoid the pump attendant as he plans to capture you. Find a free fuel hose and pull the correct lever. Then, to create a diversion so you can escape, find the tool to free the glibbers from the vacuum.

8 fuel cans

10 crates

16 waiters

13 fuel tokens

4 keys

6 space horns

9 pairs of furry dice

7 glibber traps

Ice Lands

You escaped from the space station, but your ship was hit by the station's laser cannons and you were forced to make an emergency landing in Ice Lands on Bliss. Before Glaxx started draining energy from the star, most of the planet's crops were grown here. Now it's a frozen wasteland.

Many of Glaxx's soldiers are here playing winter sports. You must find some clothes to keep warm and disguise yourselves. Find 4 pairs of snow boots, 4 pairs of goggles, 4 snow hats and 4 gooth skin coats. Don't take anything that the soldiers are wearing.

Plib's ship is damaged beyond repair and his home is on the other side of the mountains. Plib says there is a tunnel that will take you there. Find the entrance to the tunnel.

The snow is too deep to walk through, but you must reach the tunnel. There is an abandoned snow craft half buried in the snow. Find the snow craft and its handlebars, and also find a shovel to dig them out. Put them together and head for the tunnel.

Find a pot of melted gooth's cheese and 6 crusts of bread to take with you.

5 hackey masks

7 ski sticks

7 hackey pucks

7 snow boards

9 two-headed ponguins

7 hackey sticks

6 gooths

14 slalom flags

Lava Luvvies

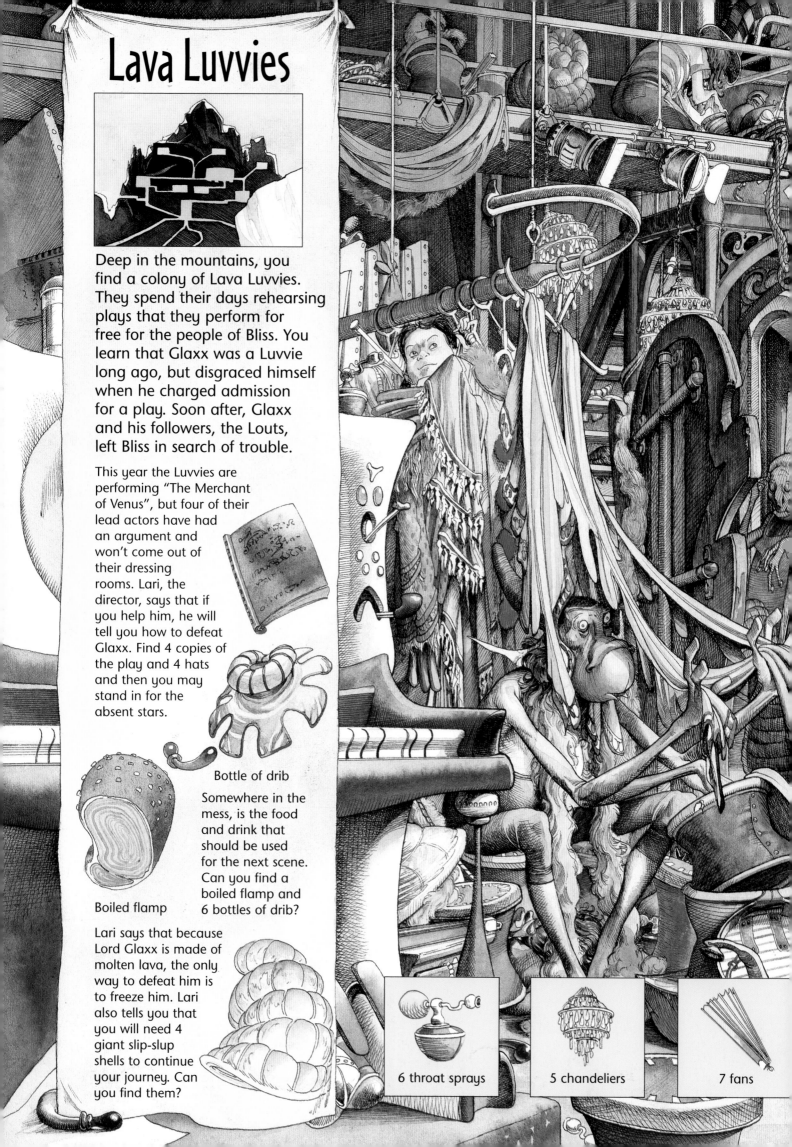

Deep in the mountains, you find a colony of Lava Luvvies. They spend their days rehearsing plays that they perform for free for the people of Bliss. You learn that Glaxx was a Luvvie long ago, but disgraced himself when he charged admission for a play. Soon after, Glaxx and his followers, the Louts, left Bliss in search of trouble.

This year the Luvvies are performing "The Merchant of Venus", but four of their lead actors have had an argument and won't come out of their dressing rooms. Lari, the director, says that if you help him, he will tell you how to defeat Glaxx. Find 4 copies of the play and 4 hats and then you may stand in for the absent stars.

Bottle of drib

Somewhere in the mess, is the food and drink that should be used for the next scene. Can you find a boiled flamp and 6 bottles of drib?

Boiled flamp

Lari says that because Lord Glaxx is made of molten lava, the only way to defeat him is to freeze him. Lari also tells you that you will need 4 giant slip-slup shells to continue your journey. Can you find them?

6 throat sprays

5 chandeliers

7 fans

13 sandbags

8 feather boas

10 hat boxes

2 pairs of binoculars

6 wigs

Loch Lung

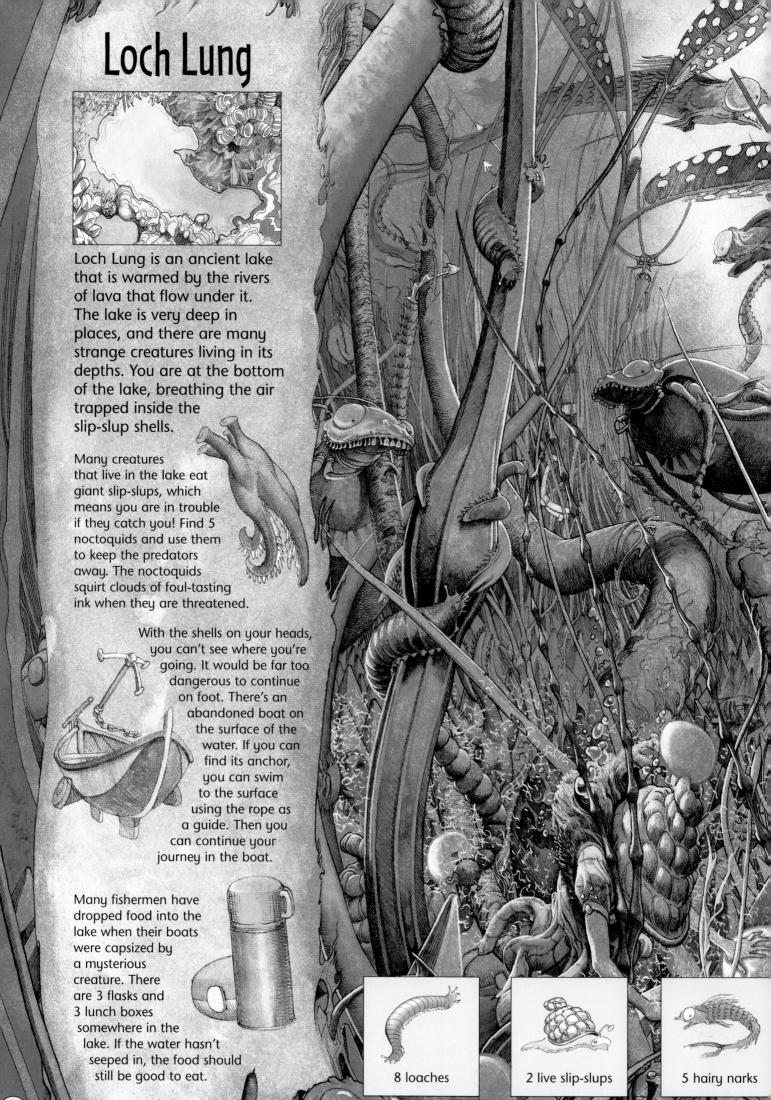

Loch Lung is an ancient lake that is warmed by the rivers of lava that flow under it. The lake is very deep in places, and there are many strange creatures living in its depths. You are at the bottom of the lake, breathing the air trapped inside the slip-slup shells.

Many creatures that live in the lake eat giant slip-slups, which means you are in trouble if they catch you! Find 5 noctoquids and use them to keep the predators away. The noctoquids squirt clouds of foul-tasting ink when they are threatened.

With the shells on your heads, you can't see where you're going. It would be far too dangerous to continue on foot. There's an abandoned boat on the surface of the water. If you can find its anchor, you can swim to the surface using the rope as a guide. Then you can continue your journey in the boat.

Many fishermen have dropped food into the lake when their boats were capsized by a mysterious creature. There are 3 flasks and 3 lunch boxes somewhere in the lake. If the water hasn't seeped in, the food should still be good to eat.

8 loaches

2 live slip-slups

5 hairy narks

5 stone fish   8 squirms   6 hooks   5 eatles   10 blobbers

Ooh Aah Forest

Everything in the Ooh Aah Forest either stings or bites. The trees and plants are so dense in this part of the forest that the cold weather on the rest of the planet still hasn't reached it.

Just one bite from an Ooh Aah moskeet will put you to sleep for a week and a day. The only way to keep the moskeets away is by grating the seeds of a special plant that grows in the forest. Find 6 seeds and the seed grater.

Grater

Seed

It is very hard to find any food that is safe to eat. The easiest thing to do is to take food from the gimmy minkeys. There are 5 gimmy minkeys eating. Find them and snatch their food

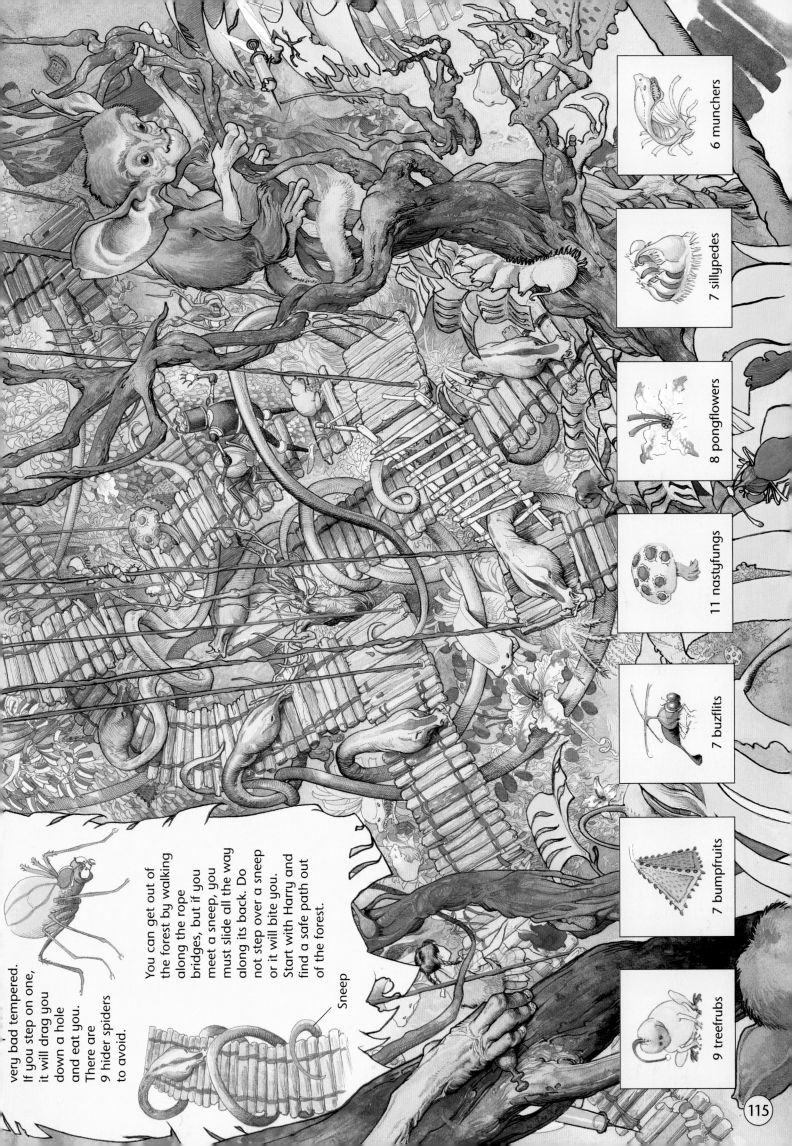

very bad tempered.
If you step on one,
it will drag you
down a hole
and eat you.
There are
9 hider spiders
to avoid.

You can get out of
the forest by walking
along the rope
bridges, but if you
meet a sneep, you
must slide all the way
along its back. Do
not step over a sneep
or it will bite you.
Start with Harry and
find a safe path out
of the forest.

Sneep

6 munchers

7 sillypedes

8 pongflowers

11 nastyfungs

7 buzflits

7 bumpfruits

9 treefrubs

Blange

You have arrived at Plib's home town which is called Blange. Everyone is trying to keep warm in the frozen food factory. Before Glaxx started draining the star's energy, the Blissters used to freeze their crops in this factory and export the food to planets all over the galaxy.

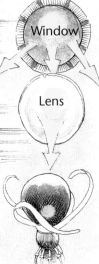

Window

Lens

Heater

The heating in the town has broken down because everything is solar powered, and the star doesn't have enough energy to make the machines work. If you can find a large magnifying lens, you may be able to concentrate enough power from the star to direct onto the solar panel that powers the factory heater.

To quick-freeze food, the Blissters used freezer cannons powered by energy crystals. The cannons would be ideal to use against the Lava Louts, along with the 6 crystals you collected earlier. There are 4 cannons and another crystal to find in the factory.

Peep

Most of the food has been eaten, but there are some frozen peeps left over. Find 6 peeps and allow them to defrost slowly near the factory heater.

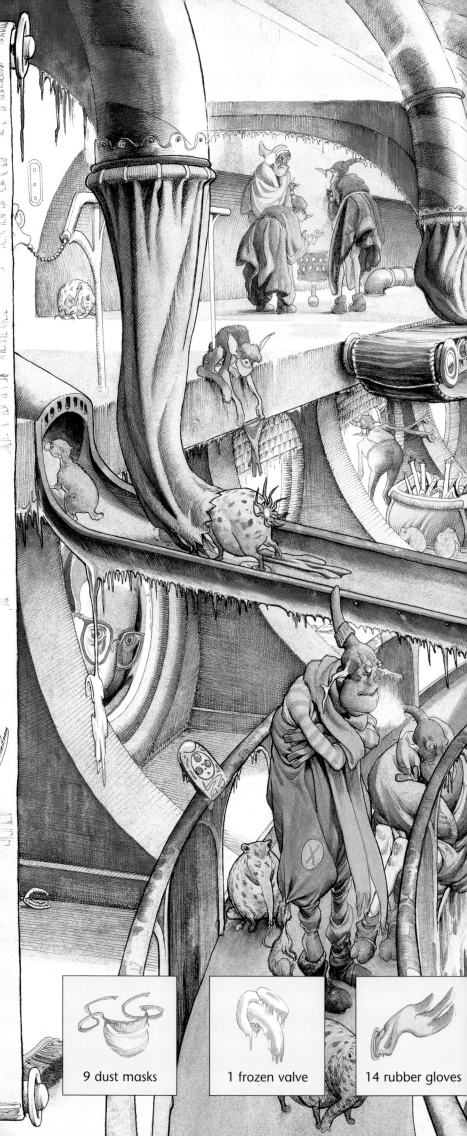

9 dust masks

1 frozen valve

14 rubber gloves

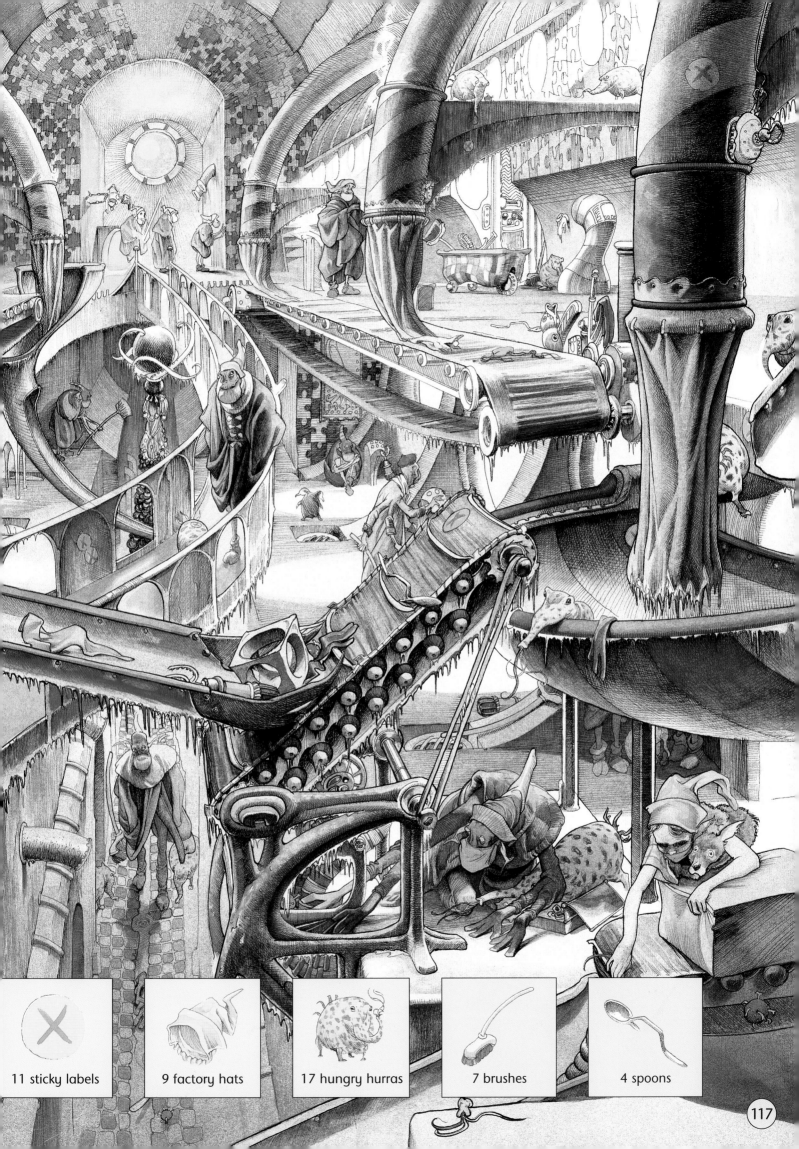

11 sticky labels

9 factory hats

17 hungry hurras

7 brushes

4 spoons

Blange Museum

The fastest and safest way to reach Glaxx's spaceship is by teleporting there. Unfortunately the town's teleporter isn't working due to the lack of energy. You have come to Blange Museum because there is a very old clockwork teleporter called the Jigger Jugger here. You may be able to make it work.

The museum is swarming with nasty flying creatures called crackacks. They must have broken a window to get in. Crackacks love to chew on old bones. Find 12 old bones and throw them out of the broken window. The crackacks will fly out after them.

The largest, smallest and strangest vegetables ever grown on Bliss are on display in the museum. Most of them have dried out and wouldn't be nice to eat, but there is one bluebibble that was put into the exhibition last week that might still be edible.

The Jigger Jugger is in the middle of the room. The key has been put away for safety. Find the key and use it to wind the machine. Then sit on the seats and think very hard about Glaxx's ship. (Don't forget to find the last 3 crystals before you go).

11 crackacks

8 saddles

5 energy bulbs

5 bendescopes

7 levers

6 poddle skulls

4 tooth pullers

11 crackack eggs

Glaxx's Ship

You've arrived in the transporter room of Glaxx's ship, but the Jigger Jugger's ancient machinery has caused the ship's own transporter to malfunction. Now it is transporting parts of Plib's and Harry's bodies around the room. You'll have to find their body parts and put them back together. Then you can freeze the Lava Louts with the freezer cannons.

Now you must shut the transporter down to stop any more Louts from coming up from the surface of the planet. There are 3 handles that control the transporter. You need to find them and pull them down.

Glaxx is in the Laser Room, draining more power from the star. To find the laser room, pick up a copy of the ship's guide. It contains useful information and a plan of the ship.

There are many cans scattered around the room, but the food in most of them tastes horrible. The pokey blubber is not too bad, though. Find 1 can of pokey blubber and a can opener.

Can opener

6 walky squawkys

5 window sprays

3 cans of lava

120

6 old meteors

8 space flies

7 cans of squeak

5 packets of bubble gum

8 ow guns

Laser Room

You have found your way to the Laser Room where the evil Lord Glaxx is draining the energy from the star with his powerful laser. You find that your freezer cannons don't have enough energy to freeze him, so you must find another way of stopping him from destroying the star completely.

First you must get Glaxx away from the laser. One of the Lava Louts' greatest fears are rock beetles which bite and crunch and chew their hard, stony skin. There are 7 beetle traps in the room. Each one contains an angry rock beetle. Find and open the traps and throw the beetles at Glaxx.

While Glaxx tries to get the beetles out of his clothes, find 4 space suits and put them on. Find and open the airlock, then hold on tight! Glaxx will be sucked out of the airlock into space where it is so cold, he will freeze and shatter into a million pieces.

Find the laser's gear shift lever. Put it into reverse and fire the laser. All the energy will transfer from the storage tanks into the star and Bliss will warm up again.

Now you can return to Bliss for a big party in the glorious sunshine before going home.

5 oil cans

10 T-pipes

21 grease monkeys

7 pressure valves   5 oily rags   6 grease cans   7 oily combs   5 valve handles

Star World 102–103

Plib 1

Jess 2

Harry 3

Plib's spaceship 4

Starburgers 5 6 7 8 9

Solarshakes 10 11 12
13 14

Space helmets 15 16 17
18 19 20 21

Roadrunners 22 23 24 25
26 27 28 29 30

Lollipops 31 32 33 34 35
36 37 38 39 40 41 42

Star World hats 43 44 45
46 47 48 49 50 51 52
53 54 55 56

Security guards 57 58 59
60 61 62 63 64 65 66

Prairie dogs 67 68 69 70
71 72 73 74 75

Balloons 76 77 78 79 80
81 82 83 84 85 86 87
88 89 90 91 92 93 94
95 96 97 98 99 100
101 102 103 104 105
106 107 108 109 110

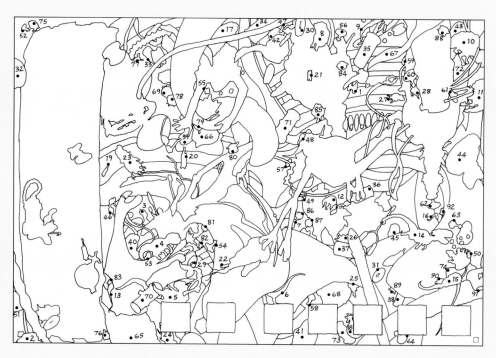

Plib's Ship 104–105

Gravity handle 1

Glibbers 2 3 4 5 6 7 8 9
10 11 12 13 14 15 16

Vacuum cleaner 17

Zoom drive 18

Zoom rods 19 20 21 22

Glimyubbers 23 24 25 26
27 28

Greeblows 29 30 31

Cans of de-icer 32 33 34
35 36 37 38

Moon boots 39 40 41 42
43 44 45

Pairs of goggles 46 47 48
49 50

Spare fuses 51 52 53 54
55 56 57 58 59 60 61
62 63 64

Travel blankets 65 66
67 68

Music cylinders 69 70 71
72 73 74

Air fresheners 75 76 77
78 79 80 81 82 83 84
85 86 87 88 89 90 91

Energy crystal 92

Space Station 106–107

Blue salads 1 2 3 4 5 6 7

Pizza slices 8 9 10 11 12
13 14 15 16 17 18 19

Fuel hose 20

Correct lever 21

Tool 22

Fuel cans 23 24 25 26 27
28 29 30

Crates 31 32 33 34 35 36
37 38 39 40

Waiters 41 42 43 44 45
46 47 48 49 50 51 52
53 54 55 56

Fuel tokens 57 58 59 60
61 62 63 64 65 66 67
68 69

Keys 70 71 72 73

Space horns 74 75 76 77
78 79

Pairs of furry dice 80 81
82 83 84 85 86 87 88

Glibber traps 89 90 91 92
93 94 95

Energy crystal 96

Button Jess should press
97

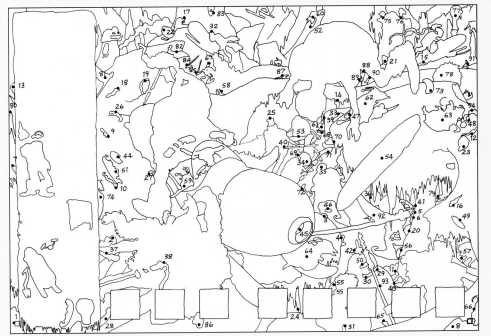

Ice Lands 108–109

Snow boots 1 2 3 4 5 6 7 8

Goggles 9 10 11 12

Snow hats 13 14 15 16

Gooth skin coats 17 18 19 20

Tunnel entrance 21

Snow craft 22

Handlebars 23

Shovel 24

Gooth's cheese 25

Crusts of bread 26 27 28 29 30 31

Hackey masks 32 33 34 35 36

Ski sticks 37 38 39 40 41 42 43

Hackey pucks 44 45 46 47 48 49 50

Snow boards 51 52 53 54 55 56 57

Ponguins 58 59 60 61 62 63 64 65 66

Hackey sticks 67 68 69 70 71 72 73

Gooths 74 75 76 77 78 79

Slalom flags 80 81 82 83 84 85 86 87 88 89 90 91 92 93

Energy crystal 94

Lava Luvvies 110–111

Copies of the play 1 2 3 4

Hats 5 6 7 8

Boiled flamp 9

Bottles of drib 10 11 12 13 14 15

Giant slip-slup shells 16 17 18 19

Throat sprays 20 21 22 23 24 25

Chandeliers 26 27 28 29 30

Fans 31 32 33 34 35 36 37

Sandbags 38 39 40 41 42 43 44 45 46 47 48 49 50

Feather boas 51 52 53 54 55 56 57 58

Hat boxes 59 60 61 62 63 64 65 66 67 68

Binoculars 69 70

Wigs 71 72 73 74 75 76

Energy crystal 77

Loch Lung 112–113

Noctoquids 1 2 3 4 5

Boat 6

Anchor 7

Flasks 8 9 10

Lunch boxes 11 12 13

Loaches 14 15 16 17 18 19 20 21

Live slip-slups 22 23

Hairy narks 24 25 26 27 28

Stone fish 29 30 31 32 33

Squirms 34 35 36 37 38 39 40 41

Hooks 42 43 44 45 46 47

Eatles 48 49 50 51 52

Blobbers 53 54 55 56 57 58 59 60 61 62

Energy crystal 63

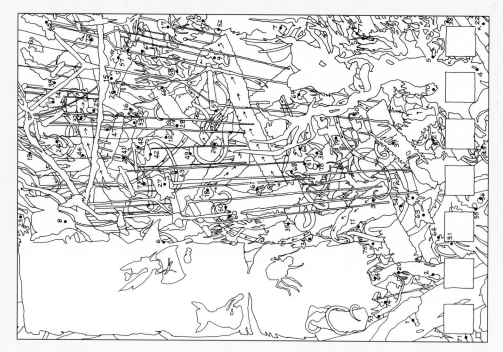

Ooh Aah Forest 114–115

Seeds 1 2 3 4 5 6

Grater 7

Gimmy monkeys (eating) 8 9 10 11 12

Hider spiders 13 14 15 16 17 18 19 20 21

Harry's route starts at 22. The arrows show his safe route out of the desert.

Treefrubs 23 24 25 26 27 28 29 30 31

Bumpfruits 32 33 34 35 36 37 38

Buzflits 39 40 41 42 43 44 45

Nastyfungs 46 47 48 49 50 51 52 53 54 55 56

Pong flowers 57 58 59 60 61 62 63 64

Sillypedes 65 66 67 68 69 70 71

Munchers 72 73 74 75 76 77

Energy crystal 78

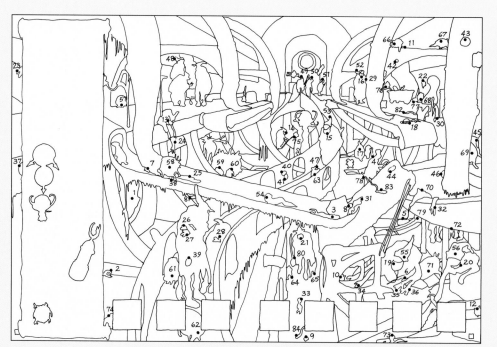

Blange 116–117

Magnifying lens 1

Freezer cannons 2 3 4 5

Energy crystal 6

Peeps 7 8 9 10 11 12

Dust masks 13 14 15 16 17 18 19 20 21

Frozen valve 22

Rubber gloves 23 24 25 26 27 28 29 30 31 32 33 34 35 36

Sticky labels 37 38 39 40 41 42 43 44 45 46 47

Factory hats 48 49 50 51 52 53 54 55 56

Hungry hurras 57 58 59 60 61 62 63 64 65 66 67 68 69 70 71 72 73

Brushes 74 75 76 77 78 79 80

Spoons 81 82 83 84

Blange Museum 118–119

Old bones 1 2 3 4 5 6 7 8 9 10 11 12

Bluebibble 13

Jigger Jugger key 14

Crackacks 15 16 17 18 19 20 21 22 23 24 25

Saddles 26 27 28 29 30 31 32 33

Energy bulbs 34 35 36 37 38

Bendescopes 39 40 41 42 43

Levers 44 45 46 47 48 49 50

Poddle skulls 51 52 53 54 55 56

Tooth pullers 57 58 59 60

Crackack eggs 61 62 63 64 65 66 67 68 69 70 71

Energy crystals 72 73 74

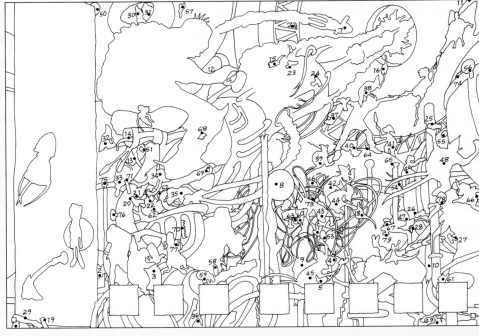

Glaxx's Ship 120–121

Plib 1 2

Harry 3 4

Transporter control
handles 5 6 7

Ship's guide 8

Pokey blubber 9

Can opener 10

Walky squawkys 11 12
13 14 15 16

Window sprays 17 18
19 20 21

Cans of lava 22 23 24

Old meteors 25 26 27
28 29 30

Space flies 31 32 33 34
35 36 37 38

Cans of squeak 39 40
41 42 43 44 45

Bubble gums 46 47 48
49 50

Ow guns 51 52 53 54
55 56 57 58

Laser Room 122–123

Beetle traps 1 2 3 4 5
6 7

Space suits 8 9 10 11

Air lock 12

Laser's gear shift lever
13

Oil cans 14 15 16 17 18

T-pipes 19 20 21 22 23
24 25 26 27 28

Grease monkeys 29 30
31 32 33 34 35 36 37
38 39 40 41 42 43 44
45 46 47 48 49

Pressure valves 50 51 52
53 54 55 56

Oily rags 57 58 59
60 61

Grease cans 62 63 64
65 66 67

Oily combs 68 69 70 71
72 73 74

Valve handles 75 76 77
78 79

Did you also notice?

~ a prairie dog fishing for food in Star World?

~ a glibber with a sweet tooth on Plib's Ship?

~ someone taking a dog for a space walk in the Space Station?

~ a snowboarding two-headed ponguin in Ice Lands?

~ a monster in Loch Lung?

~ that glibber with the sweet tooth again on Glaxx's Ship?

Goodbye!